LIFE IN OREGON COUNTRY
BEFORE THE EMIGRATION

Life in Oregon Country Before the Emigration

By CHARLES WILKES

Edited by
Richard E. Moore

The Oregon Book Society : Ashland, 1975

IN THE WILLAMETTE VALLEY

THE BARGE in which we embarked was one that usually carried freight; but it had been fitted up with seats for our use, so that we found ourselves extremely comfortable, and our jaunt was much more pleasant than if we had been confined to a small canoe. These flatbottom boats are capable of carrying three hundred bushels of wheat, and have but a small draft of water; when well manned, they are as fast as the canoes, and are exceedingly well adapted to the navigation of the river: they are also provided with large tarpawlings to protect their cargo from the weather.

From Vancouver we floated down with the current to the upper mouth of the Willamette, which we entered, and before night passed the encampment of the Rev. Jason Lee, principal of the Methodist Mission in Oregon, who was on his way to Clatsop, at the mouth of the Columbia. We stopped with him for an hour. He was accompanied by his wife, Mr. and Mrs. Whitwell, and two or three children. Their encampment was close to the river, and consisted of two small tents. Mr. Lee gave us a warm invitation to visit the settlement on the Willamette, thus forestalling our intentions to do so.

The musquitoes and sand-flies were so annoying, that we were glad to seek for higher ground to encamp on, for the purpose of escaping them.

The Willamette river is generally about one-fourth of a mile wide. For the distance of four miles from its entrance into the Columbia its banks are low, and during the rise of the latter are overflowed, its waters being backed into the Willamette. There is little current to contend with in this river during this season. After passing this low ground, the banks become high and precipitous, and are in only a few places susceptible of cultivation.

We encamped on the island* occupied by the young Americans,

---

*Swan Island, near the present site of the city of Portland.

of whom I spoke in the preceding chapter, and close to the place where they were building their vessel. The group of which it is one, is called the Oak Islands.

On landing, we were introduced to them all. They had reached the Oregon country by crossing the Rocky Mountains, a year before, and worked on the Willamette, where they first proposed to settle themselves; but they found that that was out of the question, as there was little or no prospect of their being contented, and they were now bent upon leaving the country at all hazards. Every one with whom I spoke gave them a good character, except one, and I found that, shortly after my visit, he had been turned out of the partnership.

The vessel they were building was a small schooner. One of their number having served a short time in a ship-yard in the United States, the rest were employed as his assistants, cutting timber and preparing the plank, which they procured from the cedar on the banks of the river.

I explained to them the cause of Dr. M'Laughlin's refusal to assist them, which they denied most positively. I then told them it was proper for them to deny having authorized any trick or deception, on doing which I was sure they would receive any assistance that lay in the power of Dr. M'Laughlin. This they subsequently did, and I was informed that they then received all the aid he had it in his power to give.

I tried to dissuade these young men from making their voyage; for I found, on conversing with them, that not one of them knew any thing about the sailing of a vessel or navigation. I therefore knew how great dangers they would experience on the voyage even to California, whither they intended to go, with the intention of taking sea-otter by the way on the coast of Oregon. After their arrival at San Francisco it was their plan to sell their vessel and cargo, if they were fortunate enough to obtain any, or if not, to go down the coast further, when they would cross over the country, and return by the way of Mexico or Texas.

It gave me much pleasure to see the buoyancy of spirit, so truly characteristic of our countrymen, with which they carried on their plan.

Before I left the Columbia in September, they asked me for a sea-letter for their protection; at the same time informing me that their vessel was launched, met their expectations, and was called the "Star of Oregon."*

The grove of oak on this island was beautiful, forming an extensive wood, with no undergrowth. The species that grows here is a white-oak, of very close grain. Its specific gravity is much greater than water; and it is used for the purposes to which we apply both oak and hickory. It makes excellent hoops for casks, and is the only timber of this region that is considered durable.

The next morning, I left the boat-builders, after assuring them that they should have all the assistance I could give them in their outfit.

After we had embarked, we were told by our guide, Plumondon, that he had with him saddles and bridles, and orders for horses, &c., in order that we might meet with no delay or inconvenience in our trip up the Willamette. I felt these kind attentions and the manner they were bestowed; and it gives me great pleasure to acknowledge how much we were benefited by them.

Early on the morning of the 5th, we set out for the falls of the Willamette. As they are approached, the river becomes much narrower; and the banks, which are of trap rock, more precipitous.

---

*It is said that Dr. McLoughlin also erroneously suspected these young men (Joseph Gale, Henry Wood and ex-shipbuilder Felix Hathaway) of planning a career as pirates. They put to sea for San Francisco in the *Star of Oregon* with a crew of four farmers and an Indian boy and, surviving a severe storm of several days, arrived safely and traded the vessel for 350 cattle.

This river is navigable for small vessels, even at its lowest stage, as high as the mouth of the Klackamus, three miles below its falls. In the low state of the river, there is a rapid at the Klackamus.

We reached the falls about noon, where we found the missionary station under the charge of the Rev. Mr. Waller.* The Hudson Bay Company have a trading-post here, and are packing fish, which the Indians catch in great quantities. This is said to be one of the best salmon-fisheries on the river.

There was a petty dispute between Mr. Waller and the Company, and he complained of them. It seems that the Company refuse to buy any beaver-skins, except from the hunters and trappers; and he accuses them of monopoly in consequence. The Company, on the other hand, say that they have no idea of selling goods out of their own stores, for the purpose of enabling others to enter into competition with them; and that they will spare no expense to keep the trade, as long as they can, in their own hands. This is certainly not unfair. I cannot help feeling it is quite unsuited to the life of a missionary, to be entering into trade of any kind. To embark in traffic must, I think, tend to destroy the usefulness of a missionary, or divert his attention from the great cause in which he is engaged. I am very far from attaching any blame on this account to the missionaries, whose avowed object is to teach the arts of civilization, as well as the Word of God, and I have no doubt that they are doing all in their power to promote the latter object; but I am disposed to think, that any complaints against the Hudson Bay Company for endeavouring to keep the trade in their own hands, comes with an ill grace from the members of a mission who are daily receiving the kindest attentions and hospitality from its officers.

---

*The Methodist Rev. Alvin F. Waller unsuccessfully disputed Dr. McLoughlin's claim, filed in 1829, to some lands at Oregon City. The community was known as Willamette Falls until 1842.

Mr. Waller and his wife gave us a kind welcome, and insisted upon our taking dinner with them. As they have no servants, Mrs. Waller prepared the dinner, while Mr. Waller took care of the out-door business. Though the house was built of rough materials, it was very evident that neatness and order prevailed. Her management of the home-made cooking-stove which stood in the room, claimed my admiration. At the same time she made herself quite agreeable; and although she had many, very many things to contend with, appeared quite satisfied with her lot and condition.

After we had partaken of our dinner, consisting of salmon and tea, with bread and butter, Mr. Waller took us to see the falls. On our way thither, he pointed out a log house that had been built by the agent of Mr. Slacum,* in order to secure the right of site or mill-privileges. The Hudson Bay Company have gone to considerable expense in blasting the rock for a mill-race for the same purpose; but from appearances, this work has remained untouched for several years.

The falls of Willamette are about twenty feet in height, and probably offer the best mill-sites of any place in the neighbouring country. Being at the head of navigation for sea-vessels, and near the great wheat-growing valley of the Willamette, it must be a place of great resort. A Mr. Moore, from the Western States, whom I saw on the Willamette, informed me that he had taken possession of the west side of the falls, under a purchase from an old Indian chief. Whether such titles will be recognised by the government, is already a matter of speculation in the country; and there is much talk of pre-emption rights, &c.

At the time of our visit to the falls, the salmon-fishery was at its

---

*Lieutenant William A. Slacum of the U. S. Navy was in Oregon in 1836-38 apparently to gather information which might encourage the American Government to annex the territory, and to incite the settlers to urge this. He also financed Ewing Young's first cattle-drive.

height, and was to us a novel as well as an amusing scene. The salmon leap the fall; and it would be inconceivable, if not actually witnessed, how they can force themselves up, and after a leap of from ten to twelve feet retain strength enough to stem the force of the water above. About one in ten of those who jumped, would succeed in getting by. They are seen to dart out of the foam beneath and reach about two-thirds of the height, at a single bound: those that thus passed the apex of the running water, succeed; but all that fell short, were thrown back again into the foam. I never saw so many fish collected together before; and the Indians are constantly employed in taking them. They rig out two stout poles, long enough to project over the foaming cauldron, and secure their larger ends to the rocks. On the outer end they make a platform for the fisherman to stand on, who is perched on it with a pole thirty feet long in hand, to which the net is fastened by a hoop four feet in diameter: the net is made to slide on the hoop, so as to close its mouth when the fish is taken. The mode of using the net is peculiar: they throw it into the foam as far up the stream as they can reach, and it being then quickly carried down, the fish who are running up in a contrary direction, are caught. Sometimes twenty large fish are taken by a single person in an hour; and it is only surprising that twice as many should not be caught.

The river at the falls is three hundred and fifty yards wide, and its greatest fall twenty-five feet. When the water is not very high, the rapids begin some distance above the falls. Some of the Indians are in the habit of coming down in canoes to the brink of the falls, where they secure themselves by thrusting down poles in the crevices of the rock. There they take many fish, that have succeeded in passing the lower fall, with a hook fastened to the end of a pole. These are esteemed to be of the best flavour, as they are the strongest and fattest. It is said from these places the fish can be seen very distinctly passing up, and are taken very rapidly; but

THE FISHING VILLAGE AT WILLAMETTE FALLS.

few Indians are willing or expose themselves to the risk of fishing
there. The number of Indians at the Willamette Falls during the
fishing season is about seventy, including all ages and sexes: there
are others who visit the falls in canoes for fish, which at times will
raise the number to not far from one hundred. Those fish which
are unable to get up remain some time at the falls, very much exhausted, and finally resort to the smaller streams below. Mr.
Drayton's sketch of the scene is given in the vignette.

The rocks here change their character within a few miles. Much
volcanic scoria [cinders], vesicular lava, and pudding-stone, inter-
mingled with blocks of trap, and many crystals of quartz, occur.
My attention was called to this particularly by old Mr. Moore, who
had set up his claims to the west side of the falls, communicating
to me in confidence that he intended to erect furnaces for smelting
iron, &c. Although I saw the old man some time afterwards, and
told him of his mistake, he would not believe that he had been in

[101]

error. On the rocks are to be seen large knots of lamprey eels, worming themselves up, which make them look at a little distance as if alive with snakes.

After spending some time at the falls, we returned to the house, and thence passed over to the west side of the river in a boat. Plumondon informed us that all our baggage had been transported over the portage, which is about a third of a mile in length.

On landing, we passed through an Indian village, which was absolutely swarming with fleas; a filthier place cannot be found in Oregon. Before we reached our boat, a heavy shower of rain overtook us, and gave us a good drenching; we, however, embarked for Camp Maude du Sable. We now found our progress very different from what we had made below the falls: the current was strong, and we made but little headway; our boatmen being intent upon taking advantage of the smallest eddies, we were continually crossing and recrossing the river for this purpose. The banks had become much higher and more picturesque. This part of the river is considered dangerous when the water is high, and accidents frequently occur; for this reason, the Indians in passing are still in the habit of making a propitiatory offering of some of their food, such as dried salmon or peas, in order that they may have a safe passage by. Before night we encamped just above the Stony Islands, on a barren point of land, at some height above the river, where we found several mosses in flower, which we had not met with before.

At this season of the year, the river is not high: its rise usually takes place in February and March, when it becomes very much swollen, and with its tributaries does much damage. These floods, however, are of very short duration, for the descent is so rapid that the waters are soon discharged. It was raining quite hard when we passed Camp Maude du Sable, a sandy point just at the opening out of the Willamette Valley, which was one of the points originally occupied when the river was first explored by the whites. About two miles further up the river is Champooing, eighteen miles above the falls, which we reached at about 4 P.M. Here we found a few log houses, one of which belonged to a Mr. Johnson, who gave us a hearty welcome. Mr. Johnson was formerly a trapper in the Hudson Bay Company's service, but has begun to farm here. He invited us to take up our quarters with him, and although they were not very pleasant in appearance, we thought it better to accept the invitation than to pitch our tents on the wet ground in the rain. To reach his dwelling, we passed through water over our shoes. The house had little the appearance of belonging to a white man, but his welcome made amends for many things. We were soon installed in his bed-room, where, in looking round, my eye was arrested by a print of the capture of the frigate Guerriere by the Constitution,* which led me to speak concerning it, when I found he had been in that action. This at once made us old friends, for I found him familiar with the character of all our naval men, and I had much pleasure in listening to his anecdotes, and hearing him speak in high terms of many of those officers to whom I feel personally attached. It was delightful to hear his unvarnished account of Commodore Hull's coolness and conduct in the action. Johnson asked many questions about the young officers he had known. I was equally diverted with his own adventures. Finding, after the excitement of war was over, he could not be content to lead a quiet life, he determined to adopt the business of trapping. In this he was engaged until the last few years, when he had settled himself down here, and taken an Indian girl for his wife, by whom he had several children. To the latter he said he was desirous of giving a good education, and for this purpose he had engaged old Mr. Moore, from Illinois, to pass

*The British warship *Guerrière* was defeated by the *U. S. S. Constitution* ("Old Ironsides") in a famous sea battle off Nova Scotia, in the War of 1812.

several months with him. Johnson had all the easy and independent character of a trapper; yet I could still perceive that he had hanging about him somewhat of the feeling of discipline that he had acquired in the service. His Indian wife is extremely useful in making every thing, besides taking care of the household concerns, and is rather pretty. Johnson's estimate of her was that she was worth "half a dozen civilized wives." There is little cleanliness, however, about his house, and many of the duties are left to two young male slaves, of Indian blood, but of what tribe I did not learn. Johnson's farm consists of about forty acres under cultivation: his wheat and potatoes were flourishing, and he had a tolerable kitchen-garden. He has some little stock, but complained much of the Oregon tiger, or American panther. These voracious animals are numerous and bold: the night before we arrived, they had entered the pen and killed a calf, regardless of the dogs; and an alarm was given on the night of our stay, when all the guns were in requisition, and noise enough was made in getting ready, to scare away dozens of them.

We were informed that there are plenty of elk, and deer, and that the grizzly bear is also common. The flesh of the latter animal is very much esteemed. Wild ducks and geese are quite numerous in the spring and fall, covering the rivers, lakes, and ponds.

There are four houses and three lodges in sight of Johnson's farm, whence all the neighbours called to see us. They were just the sort of men one would expect to see in such a place. One was an old man by the name of Cannon, who had been one of the party with Lewis and Clarke, and was from his own account the only remaining one in the country. He likes the country, and says he thinks there is no necessity for Dr. M'Laughlin's authority or laws to govern it.

Old Moore had some shrewdness, and was exceedingly talkative; he possessed much information in relation to the country he had passed through, which I found to correspond to what I have since

[104]

received from other sources. He had crossed the mountains the year before, and found no difficulty in making the trip. He intends to return and bring out his family, being of opinion that the country is a fine one, and exceedingly healthy, and that it will compare well with the lands of Missouri and Illinois. The great objection to the upper country, on the route by which we travelled, was the want of wood.

Another of these men was named George Gay,[1] of whom I shall speak hereafter.

We found this, as I said before, a dirty house: the people were idle and fond of lounging, and all I have yet seen are uncombed and unshaved.

These people were quite alive on the subject of laws, courts, and magistrates, including governors, judges, &c. I was here informed that a committee had been appointed to wait upon me on my arrival at the mission, to hold a consultation relative to the establishment of settled governments. Johnson, trapper-like, took what I thought the soundest view, saying that they yet lived in the bush, and let all do right, there was no necessity for laws, lawyers, or magistrates.

Having our camp equipage with us, together with plenty of provisions, our servant managed without putting him or his wife to much inconvenience; and although we passed an uncomfortable night, fighting with the fleas, yet we both agreed it was better than if we had been in our tents.

In the morning we found horses waiting, under charge of Michel La Framboise,[2] who is in the employ of the Company, and was very

---

[1] An archtype of the self-reliant frontier settler and good neighbor, Gay (among other achievements) built the first brick dwelling-house in Oregon Country. Located in the countryside on the northern boundary of Marion County, the original structure stood intact until 1937.

[2] This was the same man who served David Douglas as interpreter and guide in 1826.

happy to see us. He originally came out in the ship Tonquin, and was one of the party that landed at Astoria, where he has resided ever since, either in the employ of the Northwest or Hudson Bay Company. Michel is of low stature, and rather corpulent, but he has great energy and activity of both mind and body, indomitable courage, and all the vivacity of a Frenchman. He has travelled in all parts of the country, and says that he has a wife of high rank in every tribe, by which means he has insured his safety. From him I derived much information, and to him all parties refer as possessing the most accurate knowledge of the country. He generally has charge of a party, and was formerly engaged in trapping; but of late years passing through the country to California and back. Had it not been for his proneness to dissipation, I am informed he would have risen in the Company's service. To me he complained that he had not received what he considered his due, and that he was no better off than twenty years before, saying, "he was still Michel La Framboise, only older."

I was glad to meet with a guide of such intelligence; and having mounted our horses, we rode through the Willamette Valley. In it we passed many small farms, of from fifty to one hundred acres, belonging to the old servants of the Company, Canadians, who have settled here: they all appear very comfortable and thriving. We stopped for a few hours at the Catholic Mission, twelve miles from Champooing, to call upon the Rev. Mr. Bachelét,* to whom I had a note of introduction from Dr. M'Laughlin, and who received me with great kindness. Mr. Bachelét is here settled among his flock, and is doing great good to the settlers in ministering to their temporal as well as spiritual wants.

---

*This may have been (with exception to the spelling of the name) Rev. Francis N. Blanchet, Catholic Vicar General for Oregon, who arrived in 1838. There were notably fewer Catholic missionaries than Protestant in this region at this time.

He spoke to me much about the system of laws the minority of the settlers were desirous of establishing, but which he had objected to, and advised his people to refuse to co-operate in; for he was of opinion that the number of settlers in the Willamette Valley would not warrant the establishment of a constitution, and as far as his people were concerned there was certainly no necessity for one, nor had he any knowledge of crime having been yet committed.

Annexed to Mr. Bachelét's house is a small chapel, fully capable of containing the present congregation.

They are erecting a large and comfortable house for Mr. Bachelét, after which it is intended to extend the chapel. These houses are situated on the borders of an extensive level prairie, which is very fertile, having a rich deep alluvial soil; they also have near them a forest of pine, oak, &c. They are now occupied in turning up the fields for the first time. Mr. Bachelét informed me that it was intended to take enough of land under cultivation to supply a large community, that will be attached to the mission; for it is the intention to establish schools here, for the instruction of the Indians as well as the Canadians and other settlers. He has already ten Indian children under his care. Mr. Bachelét informed me that the mission had been established about a year, and that it had already done much good. When he first arrived all the settlers were living with Indian women, whom they have since married, and thus legalized the connexion. This was the first step he had taken towards their moral improvement, and he had found it very successful. There were about thirty Canadian families settled here, besides about twenty persons who have no fixed residence, and are labourers. The number of Indians is estimated at between four and five hundred, including all tribes, sexes, and ages. The district under Mr. Bachelét's superintendence takes in about fifty square miles, including the Willamette Valley, Faulitz [Tualatin], and Yam-Hill Plains, and extending below the Willamette Falls as

[107]

far as the Klackamus river. The number of white residents, including the missionaries of both denominations, is thought to be about sixty.

Mr. Drayton,[1] Michel, and myself, dined with Mr. Bachelét, on oatmeal porridge, venison, strawberries, and cream. This hospitality was tendered with good and kind feelings, and with a gentlemanly deportment that spoke much in his favour, and made us regret to leave his company so soon.

When we reached Michel's house he left us, finding there was no further need for his services, as we were now accompanied by Plumondon, Johnson, George Gay, and one or two other guides, with horses.

We soon after came to some American and English settlers, and then entered on the grounds of the Methodist Mission. One of the first sights that caught my eye was a patent threshing machine in the middle of the road, that seemed to have been there for a length of time totally neglected.

We rode on to the log houses which the Messrs. Lee[2] built when they first settled here. In the neighbourhood are the wheelright's and blacksmith's, together with their work-shops, belonging to the mission, and, about a mile to the east, the hospital, built by Dr. White, who was formerly attached to this mission. I was informed by many of the settlers that this gentleman had rendered very essential service to this district. His connexion with the mission was dissolved when he returned to the United States.[3]

---

[1] Mr. J. Drayton was one of the Expedition's three artists.
[2] Rev. Jason Lee and his nephew Rev. Daniel Lee. Their mission was originally located about ten miles north of the site of the present city of Salem, on the Willamette River's east bank.
[3] Physician Elijah White and his wife and child had arrived in Oregon by ship in 1837, recruited by Jason Lee. Returning East in 1840, he was appointed Indian sub-agent for Oregon and, with Lansford Hastings (of later "Hastings Cut-off" ill-fame), White in 1842 led the first sizeable emigrant train to the region.

The hospital is now used for dwellings by some of the mission-aries. It is, perhaps, the best building in Oregon, and accommodates at present four families: it is a well-built frame edifice, with a double piazza in front. Mr. Abernethy[1] and his wife entertained us kindly. He is the secular agent of the mission. Order and neat-ness prevail in their nice apartments, where they made us very comfortable, and gave us such hospitality as we should receive at home. It seemed an out-of-the-way place to find persons of delicate habits, struggling with difficulties such as they have to encounter, and overcoming them with cheerfulness and good temper.

Near the hospital are two other houses, built of logs, in one of which Dr. Babcock, the physician of the mission, lives.[2]

We paid Dr. Babcock a visit in the evening, and found him com-fortably lodged. He stated to me that the country was healthy, although during the months of August and September they were subject to fever and ague on the low grounds, but in high and dry situations he believed they would be free from it. A few other dis-eases existed, but they were of a mild character, and readily yielded to simple remedies. He is also of opinion that the fever and ague becomes milder each season, as the individuals become acclimated.

The lands of the Methodist Mission are situated on the banks of the Willamette river, on a rich plain adjacent to fine forests of oak and pine. They are about eight miles beyond the Catholic Mission, consequently eighteen miles from Champooing, in a southern direc-tion. Their fields are well enclosed, and we passed a large one of wheat, which we understood was self-sown by the last year's crop, which had been lost through neglect. The crop so lost amounted to

---

[1] George Abernethy, who later became governor of the Oregon territory 1845-49, in the provisional government period.

[2] Dr. Ira Babcock was soon to be elected "supreme judge" by the indepen-dent settlers, serving from 1841 to 1843 and succeeding Ewing Young as their leader.

nearly a thousand bushels, and it is supposed that this year's crop will yield twenty-five bushels to the acre. About all the premises of this mission there was an evident want of the attention required to keep things in repair, and an absence of neatness that I regretted much to witness. We had the expectation of getting a sight of the Indians on whom they were inculcating good habits and teaching the word of God; but with the exception of four Indian servants, we saw none since leaving the Catholic Mission. On inquiring, I was informed that they had a school of twenty pupils, some ten miles distant, at the mill; that there were but few adult Indians in the neighbourhood; and that their intention and principal hope was to establish a colony, and by their example to induce the white settlers to locate near those over whom they trusted to exercise a moral and religious influence.

A committee of five, principally lay members of the mission, waited upon me to consult and ask my advice relative to the establishment of laws, &c. After hearing attentively all their arguments and reasons for this change, I could see none sufficiently strong to induce the step. No crime appears yet to have been committed, and the persons and property of settlers are secure. Their principal reasons appear to me to be, that it would give them more importance in the eyes of others at a distance, and induce settlers to flock in, thereby raising the value of their farms and stock. I could not view this subject in such a light, and differed with them entirely as to the necessity or policy of adopting the change.

1st. On account of their want of right, as those wishing for laws were, in fact, a small minority of the settlers.

2d. That these were not yet necessary even by their own account.

3d. That any laws they might establish would be a poor substitute for the moral code they all now followed, and that evil-doers would not be disposed to settle near a community entirely opposed to their practices.

[110]

4th. The great difficulty they would have in enforcing any laws, and defining the limits over which they had control, and the discord this might occasion in their small community.

5th. They not being the majority, and the larger part of the population being Catholics, the latter would elect officers of their party, and they would thus place themselves entirely under the control of others.

6th. The unfavourable impressions it would produce at home, from the belief that the missions had admitted that in a community brought together by themselves they had not enough of moral force to control it and prevent crime, and therefore must have recourse to a criminal code.

From my own observation and the information I had obtained, I was well satisfied that laws were not needed, and were not desired by the Catholic portion of the settlers. I therefore could not avoid drawing their attention to the fact, that after all the various officers they proposed making were appointed, there would be no subjects for the law to deal with. I further advised them to wait until the government of the United States should throw its mantle over them. These views, I was afterwards told, determined a postponement of their intentions.

Dr. Babcock and others, myself and officers, were tendered an invitation from the American settlers of the Willamette, to partake of a 4th of July dinner with them, which I was obliged to decline, on account of the various duties that pressed upon us.

The next day the gentlemen of the mission proposed a ride to what they term "the Mill," distant about nine miles, in a southeast direction.

We passed, in going thither, several fine prairies, both high and low. The soil on the higher is of a gravelly or light nature, while on the lower it is a dark loam, intermixed with a bluish clay. The prairies are at least one-third greater in extent than the forest: they

[111]

were again seen carpeted with the most luxuriant growth of flowers, of the richest tints of red, yellow, and blue, extending in places a distance of fifteen to twenty miles.

The timber we saw consisted of the live and white oak, cedar, pine, and fir.

We reached "the Mill" by noon, which consists of a small grist and saw mill on the borders of an extensive prairie. They are both under the same roof, and are worked by a horizontal wheel. The grist-mill will not grind more than ten bushels a day; and during the whole summer both mills are idle, for want of water, the stream on which they are situated being a very small one, emptying into the Willamette. We found here two good log houses, and about twenty lay members, mechanics, of the mission under Mr. Raymond, who is the principal at the mills. There are, besides, about twenty-five Indian boys, who, I was told, were not in a condition to be visited or inspected. Those whom I saw were nearly grown up, ragged and half-clothed, lounging about under the trees. Their appearance was any thing but pleasing and satisfactory; and I must own I was greatly disappointed, for I had been led to expect that order and neatness at least would have been found among them, considering the strong force of missionaries engaged here.

From the number of persons about the premises, this little spot had the air and stir of a new secular settlement; and I understood that it is intended to be the permanent location of the mission, being considered more healthy than the bank of the Willamette. The missionaries, as they told me, have made individual selections of lands to the amount of one thousand acres each, in prospect of the whole country falling under our laws.

We received an invitation from Mr. Raymond to take dinner, which we accepted; previous to which I rode about two miles to the situation selected by the Rev. Mr. Hines, in company with that gentleman. On our way, he pointed out to me the site selected for the seminary, &c. We found Mr. Hines's family encamped under some oak trees, in a beautiful prairie, to which place he had but just removed; he intended putting up his house at once, and they had the ordinary comforts about them. We returned, and found the table well spread with good things, consisting of salmon, pork, potted cheese, strawberries and cream, and nice hot cakes, and an ample supply for the large company.

We were extremely desirous of obtaining information relative to the future plans of these missionaries as to teaching and otherwise forwarding the civilization of the Indian boys; but from all that we could learn from the missionaries, as well as lay members, my impression was that no fixed plan of operations has yet been digested; and I was somewhat surprised to hear them talking of putting up extensive buildings for missionary purposes, when it is fully apparent that there is but a very limited field for spiritual operations in this part of the country. The number now attached and under tuition are probably all that can be converted, and it does not exceed the number of those attached to the mission. I was exceedingly desirous of drawing their attention to the tribes of the north, which are a much more numerous and hardier race, with a healthy climate. It is true that a mission station has been established at Nisqually, but they are doing nothing with the native tribes, and that post is only on the borders of many larger tribes to the northward. As the holders of a charge, committed to their hands by a persevering and enlightened class of Christians at home, who are greatly interested in their doings and actions, they will be held responsible for any neglect in the great cause they have undertaken to advance, and in which much time and money have already been spent.

That all may judge of the extent of this field of missionary labours, I will enumerate the numbers of Indians within its limits. Nisqually, two hundred; Clatsop, two hundred and nine; Chinooks,

[113]

two hundred and twenty; Kilamukes, four hundred; Callapuyas, six hundred; Dalles, two hundred and fifty: say in all this district, two thousand Indians; and this field is in part occupied by the Catholics, as I have before stated. Of these, the Methodist missionaries have under their instruction, if so it may be called, twenty-five at the Willamette station; at the Dalles, and occasionally on the Klackamus river, are the only places where divine service is attempted. I would not have it understood that by these remarks I have any desire to throw blame on those who direct or are concerned in this missionary enterprise, or to make any imputations on the labourers; but I feel it a duty I owe my countrymen, to lay the truth before them, such as we saw it. I am aware that the missionaries come out to this country to colonize, and with the Christian religion as their guide and law, to give the necessary instruction, and hold out inducements to the Indians to quit their wandering habits, settle, and become cultivators of the soil. This object has not been yet attained in any degree, as was admitted by the missionaries themselves; and how it is to be effected without having constantly around them large numbers, and without exertions and strenuous efforts, I am at a loss to conceive. I cannot but believe that the same labour and money which have been expended here, would have been much more appropriately and usefully spent among the tribes about the Straits of Juan de Fuca, who are numerous, and fit objects for instruction.

At the Rev. Mr. Hines's I had another long conversation relative to the laws, &c. The only instance (which speaks volumes for the good order of the settlers), of any sort of crime being committed since the foundation of the settlement, was the stealing of a horse; and a settler who had been detected stealing his neighbour's pigs, by enticing them to his house, dropping them into his cellar, where they were slaughtered and afterwards eaten. The theft was discovered by the numbers of bones frequently found around his premises. He was brought to a confession, and compelled to pay the value of the stolen hogs, simply by the force of public opinion.

We took leave of Mr. Raymond and his party, wishing them success in their labours, and rode back over the fine prairies at a full gallop, in the direction that seemed most convenient to save us distance. We stopped for a short time to take leave of Mr. and Mrs. Abernethy, and then passed to the site of the old mission on the banks of the Willamette. The river here makes a considerable bend, and has undermined and carried away its banks to some extent: a short distance beyond, it is making rapid inroads into the rich soil of these bottom lands. The log houses have the character that all old log houses acquire, and I was warned, if I desired to pass a comfortable night, to avoid them.

This is the usual place of crossing the river, which is too deep to be forded, and about two hundred yards wide. Its banks were twenty feet high, and composed of stratified layers of alluvium. On the shore of the river, which consists of a shingle beach some two hundred feet wide, are to be found cornelians, agates, and chalcedony, among the loose pieces of basalt of which it is composed. The current was found to run at the rate of three miles an hour, although the water was said to be low. An old canoe was procurred, in which we passed over, while one of the horses was led, and swam by its side: the rest were driven into the water, and followed to the opposite side. Here we met George Gay, who was travelling with his Indian wife: he told us that he would join us on our trip to the Yam Hills, which we proposed to make the next day.

We found our camp established by Plumondon, near the residence of Mr. O'Neill, formerly the property of the Rev. Mr. Leslie: it lies about a mile from the river, in a pretty, oval prairie, containing about three or four hundred acres, with a fine wood encircling it. Sixty of these are under cultivation; about forty in wheat, that was growing luxuriantly.

[115]

Three years since, O'Neill came to the valley with only a shirt to his back, as he expressed it: he began by working part of this farm, and obtained the loan of cattle and other articles from Dr. M'Laughlin, all of which he has, from the natural increase of his stock and out of his crops, since repaid. He has bought the farm, has two hundred head of stock, horses to ride on, and a good suit of clothes, all earned by his own industry; and he says it is only necessary for him to work one month in the year to make a living: the rest of the time he may amuse himself. He spoke in the highest terms of Dr. M'Laughlin, and the generous aid he had afforded him in the beginning. This farm is the best we have seen, in every respect; and it is not only well arranged, but has many advantages from its location. The success of O'Neill is a proof of what good education and industrious habits will do, and it is pleasing to see the happiness and consideration they produce. Mr. O'Neill is also a mechanic, and has gained much of his wealth in that way: he ploughs and reaps himself, and is assisted by a few Indians, whom he has the tact to manage. He has a neat kitchen-garden, and every thing that a person in his situation can desire.

The Rev. Mr. Leslie, who lives with O'Neill, invited us to the hospitality of his roof, but we preferred our camp to putting him to any inconvenience.

The next day (9th of June) we started for the Yam Hills, which divide the valleys of the Willamette and Faulitz. They are of but moderate elevation: the tops are easily reached on horseback, and every part of them which I saw was deemed susceptible of cultivation. The soil is a reddish clay, and bears few marks of any wash from the rains. These hills are clothed to the very top with grass, and afford excellent pasturage for cattle, of which many were seen feeding on them. On our route through the Yam Hills, we passed many settlers' establishments. From their top, the view is not unlike that from Mount Holyoke, in Massachusetts, and the

[116]

country appears as if it were as much improved by the hand of civilization. The oak trees sprinkled over the hills and bottoms have a strong resemblance to the apple orchards. The extent of country we looked over is from twenty-five to thirty miles, all of which is capable of being brought to the highest state of cultivation. There are in truth few districts like that of the valley of the Faulitz [Tualatin].

We passed one or two brick-kilns, and finally reached the new residence of George Gay, one of the most remote on this side of the river. George had reached home with his wife and two children not long before us. His dwelling was to all appearance a good shanty, which contains all his valuables. George is of that lazy kind of lounging figure so peculiar to a backwoodsman or Indian. He has a pretty and useful Indian wife, who does his bidding, takes care of his children and horses, and guards his household and property. The latter is not bulky, for superfluities with George are not to be found, and when he and his wife and children are seen travelling, it is manifest that his all is with him. George is a useful member of society in this small community: he gelds and marks cattle, breaks horses in, and tames cows for milking, assists in finding and driving cattle,—in short, he undertakes all and every sort of singular business; few things are deemed by him impossibilities; and lastly, in the words of one of the settlers, "George is not a man to be trifled or fooled with." I felt, when I had him for my guide, that there were few difficulties he could not overcome. He is full as much of an Indian in habits as a white man can be. He told me he bore the Indians no love, and is indeed a terror to them, having not unfrequently applied Lynch law to some of them with much effect. The account he gave of himself is, that he was born of English parents, but became, before he had grown up, more than half Indian, and was now fully their match. I will add, that he is quite equal to them in artifice. He passes for the best lasso-thrower

[117]

in the country, and is always ready to eat, sleep, or frolic: his wife and children are to him as his trappings. He has with all this many good points about him. I have seen him, while travelling with me, dart off for half a mile to assist a poor Indian boy who was unable to catch his horse, lasso the horse, put the boy on, and return at full gallop. All this was done in a way that showed it to be his every-day practice; and his general character throughout the settlement is, that George is ever ready to help those in trouble.

On our return towards the road, we passed the farm of one of Dr. M'Laughlin's sons,* who has settled here, and has an extensive portion of the prairie fenced in. This part of Willamette Valley is a prolonged level, of miles in extent, circumscribed by the woods, which have the appearance of being attended to and kept free from undergrowth. This is difficult to account for, except through the agency of fire destroying the seeds. The Indians are in the habit of burning the country yearly, in September, for the purpose of drying and procuring the seeds of the sunflower, which they are thus enabled to gather with more ease, and which form a large portion of their food. That this is the case appears more probable from the fact that since the whites have had possession of the country, the undergrowth is coming up rapidly in places.

In passing through the Willamette, I had a good opportunity of contrasting the settlers of different countries; and, while those of French descent appeared the most contented, happy, and comfortable, those of the Anglo-Saxon race showed more of the appearance of business, and the "go-ahead" principle so much in vogue at home.

The most perfect picture of content I saw was a French Canadian by the name of La Bonte, on the Yam Hill river, who had been a long time in the service of the Hudson Bay Company. This man was very attentive to us, and assisted in getting our horses across the

---

*Possibly David McLoughlin, born in 1824.

river, which, though but a few rods wide, is yet deep and attended with much difficulty in passing.

The sudden rises of this river are somewhat remarkable and difficult to be accounted for, as there does not appear from the face of the country to be much ground drained by it. The perpendicular height of the flood is, at times, as much as thirty feet, which was marked very distinctly on the trees growing on its banks.

Having heard that the farm of the late Mr. Young* was the most beautiful spot in this section of the country, I determined to visit it, and for this purpose crossed the Yam Hills again. When we reached the top, we again had a view of the Faulitz Plains, which were highly picturesque. The hills here were covered, as we had found them before, with wall-flowers, lupines, scilla, and quantities of ripe strawberries. Mr. Young's farm is situated in a valley, running east and west, which seems to unite that of Willamette and Faulitz. The situation did not meet my high-raised expectations, though it is fine. Mr. Young was one of the first pioneers and settlers in this country and met with much difficulty. At one time he was desirous of establishing a distillery, but through the influence of Mr. Slacum, who was on a visit to Oregon as an agent of our government, he relinquished the idea, notwithstanding he had already incurred considerable expense.

Mr. Young was, at the time, of opinion that unless they had cattle, to which he believed the country was well adapted, they never could succeed in creating a successful settlement, and it was necessary to go to considerable expense to obtain them from California,

*Veteran mountain-man and fur-trader Ewing Young arrived in Oregon from California in 1834 and by 1840 had become the most prosperous settler in the Willamette district due to his ventures in cattle-drives from California. His home was in the Chehalem valley. His death without known heirs in 1841 resulted in a temporary government being formed and headed by Dr. Babcock, to dispose of his estate. The proceeds were used, somewhat surprisingly, to build a jail.

as the Hudson Bay Company, or rather the Puget Sound Company, would not part with any. Mr. Slacum generously offered to advance the money necessary, and to give as many Americans as desired it, a free passage to San Francisco, in California, there to purchase stock and to drive them through to the Willamette. This was accordingly done, and after many difficulties, the cattle reached the Willamette in 1839. Mr. Young took charge of the share of Mr. Slacum, which then amounted to twenty-three. Previous to our arrival on the Northwest Coast, we heard from the United States of the death of Mr. Slacum, and on our arrival there that of Mr. Young was also made known to me. The funds and property of Mr. Young, by general consent of the settlers, were put into the hands of the Rev. Mr. Leslie, who acted as administrator, and informed me that at the division of Mr. Young's cattle, eighty-six had been put aside as the share of Mr. Slacum, after the proportion of loss and accidents had been deducted, making the increase in four years, sixty-three. Of these cattle no other care had ever been taken than to drive them into the pens for protection at night. Mr. Slacum's share was subsequently sold at the request of his nephew, who was a midshipman on board my ship, to Dr. M'Laughlin for eight hundred and sixty dollars—ten dollars a head.

The Willamette is now, through the interest felt and advances made by Mr. Slacum, well supplied with cattle, which are fast increasing in numbers.

We found the farm of Mr. Young very much out of order, although I understood that two persons had been put in charge of it on wages at one dollar a day. The farm-house at which we stopped was entirely open, and every thing seemed to be going fast to ruin. Johnson, in hunting about the premises, found a sick man, a native of the Sandwich Islands, lying in a bunk. In a small kitchen half a pig was hanging by its hind legs; roasting over a slow fire; and every thing seemed in confusion. We did not stay long, but rode on to his saw-mill, which we found in ruins. It was badly located, although erected at much expense, for there was little timber of value in the neighbourhood. Shortly after Mr. Young's death the mill-dam was washed away, and there was no money to erect it again, even if it had been thought desirable to do so. We found it wholly deserted. I was desirous of having some further search made for the bones of a mastodon, parts of whose skeleton had been obtained by Captain Goach, master of a small vessel engaged in the salmon-fishery, a few months before our arrival. On the locality being pointed out, I found that the mass of the dam and other alluvial deposits had been heaped upon the place, and created such an obstruction as would have rendered their removal an herculean task, and have required some weeks' labour.

Neither I nor my officers had time to spare to accomplish this task; besides, it was very probable that the bones, which had been represented to me as nearly denuded prior to the flood, had been washed away and lost. The bank in which the bones were found is composed of red marl and gravel.

After leaving the mill we had a long ride before us; for it was our intention to reach Champooing before dark. The country, as we approached that place, became much more thickly settled, and the ground stony. Before dark we reached a deserted house belonging to George Gay, opposite to Champooing, and formerly occupied by Mr. Young. Finding the stream difficult to cross, we determined to take up our quarters in this house. About two miles from our stopping-place, we passed some salt springs, to which the cattle and game resort in great numbers: they are strongly saline, and cover a considerable extent of ground. This is considered, as Johnson informed me, the best grazing ground for their cattle.

In consequence of the baggage-horses and party losing their way, they did not reach the camp until near midnight.

Shortly after our arrival George Gay was employed "to break

in," as he called it, a cow for milking! This operation, as performed by George, however necessary, was not calculated to raise him in any one's opinion, and therefore I shall not venture upon a description, farther than to say that the treatment the poor beast received was in my opinion as unnecessary as it was cruel.

In the evening, we had a visit from Mr. Moore and several of the other neighbours, and I was much amused with the various accounts they gave of their trappers' life. I must here express the correct views they entertained relative to the introduction of spirits into the settlement. To my surprise, they seemed to be of an unanimous opinion that spirituous liquors would soon destroy them; and since Mr. Slacum's visit they have entered into an agreement among themselves to forego their use. It is a wise determination, and as long as adhered to the country will thrive. But should this pest be introduced, the vice of drunkenness will probably reach a height unknown elsewhere; for such is the ease with which a livelihood is gained here, that persons may be supported, and indeed grow rich, in idleness. According to the inhabitants, one month in a year of labour is all that is required for a comfortable support. This labour consists in preparing the ground, putting the seed into it, and when it is ripe, reaping the harvest. Cattle, as I have before said, require no protection or care except to guard them from the wolves. Two-thirds of the time of the settlers is consequently at their own disposal; and unless education, with its moral influence, is attended to strictly in this young settlement, these very advantages will prove its curse. On the missionaries who have settled here will depend in a great measure the future character of the inhabitants; and on them also will rest the responsibility of maintaining the morals, as well as superintending the education, of the rising population. I trust they will both see and feel the great necessity of that strict attention to their duties necessary to insure success.

In the morning, before dawn, the two Indian boys belonging to

Johnson came over to our hut for the purpose of looking for their milk-pans. Unknown to us, we had laid on its side, for a seat, a cupboard which contained them. This the boys came in search of, and in their haste awoke Mr. Drayton, who naturally thought they intended to steal some of our things: he accordingly pelted them with our boots and shoes, and all other articles that came to hand. This aroused us all, when a general outcry was raised, and the Indian boys made a precipitate retreat, not, however, before they had secured one of the objects of their search.

After breakfast, we crossed the river to Johnson's, and I was, on this second visit, more impressed with the filth, both in and out doors than before.

It was now determined that Mr. Drayton should take the boat down the river, and that I should pass through the eastern part of the Willamette Valley on horseback, to reach the falls by dark. This George Gay said could be easily done, with fresh and good horses. Taking him as a guide, I set off, and after passing a few miles, we crossed a low ridge of rough rocky ground, of trap formation, about a mile wide: it was well wooded with pines and firs. After passing the ridge, we again entered on fine prairies, part of the farm of Dr. Bailey.* This was one of the most comfortable I had yet seen, and was certainly in the neatest order. Dr. Bailey had married one of the girls who came out with the missionaries, and the mistress of the establishment was as pleasing as it was well conducted. Dr. Bailey desiring to accompany us to the falls, I gladly concluded to await their dinner, and before it was served had an opportunity of looking about the premises. The locality resembles the prairies I have so often spoken of, but there was something in the arrangements of the farm that seemed advanced beyond the other settle-

---

*Probably Dr. William J. Bailey, whose wife Margaret also wrote an interesting, presumably autobiographical work entitled *The Grains; or Passages in the Life of Ruth Rover.*

ments of the country. The garden was, in particular, exceedingly well kept, and had in it all the best vegetables of our own country. This was entirely the work of Mrs. Bailey, whose activity could not rest content until it was accomplished. She had followed the mission as a teacher, until she found there was no field for labour. She had been in hope that the great missionary field to the north, of which I have before spoken, would be occupied; but this being neglected, she had left them.

Dr. Bailey had been the practising physician of the mission. He had been several years in the country, and was one of a party that, while passing through to California, was attacked by the Indians in their camp, and nearly all murdered. Dr. Bailey, after being severely wounded, made his escape, and returned to the Willamette; but he bears the marks of several wounds on his head and face. He spoke well of the country, considers it fruitful, and healthy for white men; and that it would be so for the Indians, if they could be persuaded to take care of themselves. The ague and fever, though common on the low prairies, was not of a dangerous type, and after the first attack, those of subsequent years were less violent, even if it did occur, which was rare. The climate, however, was very destructive to the Indians, of whom at least one-fourth died off yearly.

When an Indian is sick, and considered beyond moving, he is poisoned by the medicine-man; for which purpose a decoction of the wild cucumber (Bryonia) is given him. Some of the roots of this plant grow to a very large size; and I saw some at Mr. Waller's three feet long by twelve inches in diameter.

Dr. Bailey also related to me an anecdote of Mr. Farnham,* who

*Lawyer Thomas Jefferson Farnham, a leader of the "Peoria Party" of Illinois emigrants to Oregon in 1839, stayed with the Baileys while preparing a memorial extolling the region, to be sent to Congress. Shortly afterward, without logical explanation, he returned East and published a widely-read news article "Oregon Bubble Burst" in which he decried the whole Pacific Northwest. Later, he produced a highly successful book about his overland journey.

has written upon Oregon. A few days before the latter left the country, they were lost in the woods, and were obliged to pass a cold and dark night up to their ankles in mire: this the Doctor thought had cured his enthusiasm; and the first news he received of him was his violent attack upon the country on which, a few months before, he had written so strong a panegyric.

The next farm I stopped at was that of Mr. Walker,* who came from Missouri, with all his family, last year: he did not like the country, and wished to go to California by the first opportunity. His principal objection, he told me, was to the climate, which was too wet for business. He said that the land was good, but only for crops of small grain, which there is no market for, nor is there a probability of one for some time. Indian corn cannot be raised: it was, however, a first-rate grazing country. He was a good specimen of a border-man, and appeared to think nothing of a change of domicile, although he is much past the middle age, with grown-up sons and daughters around him. He intended to go to California, and if the country did not please him, he would travel home by way of Mexico. His family consisted of eight or ten persons.

George Gay now thought it proper to notify me that we ought not to delay any longer, as we had to cross the Powder river, and he did not know the state it was in. After a hard gallop, we reached that stream at the usual fording-place. We, however, found that it was entirely filled with drift-wood, and impassable at that place for our horses. This difficulty was soon obviated, for while we were transporting the saddles, &c., across the raft of timber, he had searched out a place where the horses might cross, and dashed in

---

*Joel Walker, whose wife and children were the first family to cross the plains solely for the purpose of settling on the west coast, arrived in 1840. He later joined an exploring party which Lieutenant Wilkes sent from the Willamette to California, and was employed for a time by John Sutter at Sutter's Fort. Joel was the brother of Joseph Reddeford Walker, the discoverer of Yosemite Valley.

on one of them, while we drove the others into the river. We were soon mounted again, and on our way. This stream is about four hundred feet wide, and then about twenty feet deep. Quantities of large and fine timber were locked together, until they entirely covered the surface.

The country now became exceedingly rough, overgrown with brushwood, and in places wet and miry. It was chiefly covered with heavy pine timber. From Dr. Bailey I learned that the small prairies we occasionally passed were not capable of cultivation, owing to their being flooded after a few hours of rain.

A few miles further on we passed the Little Powder river, which was termed fordable, though the horses were obliged to swim it, after which Gay gave me a specimen of his rapid mode of riding. Having made up my mind to follow, I kept after him, and on my arrival at the falls could not help congratulating myself that we had reached our destination in safety, for the last few miles of the route was a sort of break-neck one.

At the falls I found Mr. Drayton comfortably encamped, and Mr. and Mrs. Waller again pressed us to partake of their hospitality. I occupied the evening in getting my usual observations for latitude and time.

Mr. Drayton desiring to stay a longer time at the falls, to procure as many specimens of fish as he could, and make drawings, I determined to return to Vancouver without him; which I did by the following day at sunset. On the way I stopped at the boat-builders' camp, who I found had made great progress in their undertaking, and appeared to work with great unanimity.

At Vancouver, I was again kindly made welcome by Dr. M'Laughlin, Mr. Douglass, and the officers of the establishment. During my absence, Mr. Peter Ogden, chief factor of the northern district, had arrived with his brigade. The fort had, in consequence, a very different appearance from the one it bore when I left it. I was exceedingly amused with the voyageurs of the brigade, who were to be seen lounging about in groups, decked in gay feathers, ribands, &c., full of conceit, and with the flaunting air of those who consider themselves the beau-ideal of grace and beauty; full of frolic and fun, and seeming to have nothing to do but to attend to the decorations of their persons and seek for pleasure; looking down with contempt upon those who are employed about the fort, whose sombre cast of countenance and business employments form a strong contrast to these jovial fellows.

Mr. Ogden has been thirty-two years in this country, and consequently possesses much information respecting it; having travelled nearly all over it. He resides at Fort St. James, on Stuart's Lake, and has six posts under his care.

The northern section of the country he represents as not susceptible of cultivation, on account of the proximity of the snowy mountains, which cause sudden changes, even in the heat of summer, that would destroy the crops.

His posts are amply supplied with salmon from the neighbouring waters, that empty themselves into the sounds on the coast. These fish are dried, and form the greatest part of the food of those employed by the Company during the whole year. Their small-stores of flour, &c., are all carried from Colville and Vancouver. Furs are very plenty in the northern region, and are purchased at low prices from the Indians: his return, this year, was valued at one hundred thousand dollars, and this, he informed me, was much less than the usual amount.

On the other hand, the southern section of this country, I was here informed, was scarcely worth the expense of an outlay for a party of trappers.

This southern country, as will be seen from what has been already stated, is very well adapted to the raising of cattle and sheep: of the former, many have been introduced by parties, which trap on their

[127]

way thither and return with cattle. Although there were but a few head of them four or five years before, in 1841 there were upwards of ten thousand. The whole country is particularly adapted to grazing, which, together with the mildness of the climate, must cause this region to become, in a short time, one of the best-stocked countries in the world.

The price of cattle may be quoted at ten dollars a head; but those that are broken in for labour, or milch-cows, command a higher price; and in some places in the Willamette Valley they have been sold for the enormous price of eighty dollars. Every endeavour is made to keep the price of cattle up, as labour is usually paid for in stock.

The price of labour for a mechanic may be set down at from two dollars and a half, to three dollars a day; and there is much difficulty to procure them even at that rate. The wages for a common labourer is one dollar per day. The price of wheat is fixed at sixty-two and a half cents per bushel by the Company; for which any thing but spirits may be drawn from the stores, at fifty per cent. advance on the London cost. This is supposed, all things taken into consideration, to be equal to one dollar and twelve cents per bushel; but it is difficult for the settlers so to understand it, and they are by no means satisfied with the rate. There is a description of currency here, called beaver money; which seems to be among the whites what blankets are among the Indians. The value of the currency may be estimated from the fact that a beaver-skin represents about two dollars throughout the territory.

In speaking of the Willamette Valley, I have viewed its advantages for raising crops, pasturage of stock, and the facilities of settlers becoming rich. There is, however, one objection to its ever becoming a large settlement, in consequence of the interruption of the navigation of its rivers in the dry season; which renders it difficult to get to a market, as well as to receive supplies.

[128]

The salmon-fishery may be classed as one of the great sources of wealth, for it affords a large amount of food at a very low price, and of the very best quality: it does not extend above the falls. I found it impossible to obtain any data to found a calculation of the quantity taken, but it cannot be short of eight hundred barrels; and this after the Indian manner of catching them, as before described. The finest of the salmon are those caught nearest the sea.

The settlers and Indians told us that the salmon as they pass up the river become poorer, and when they reach the tributaries of the upper Columbia, they are exceedingly exhausted, and have their bodies and heads much disfigured and cut, and their tails and fins worn out by contact with the rocks. Many of the salmon in consequence die: these the Indians are in the habit of drying for food, by hanging them on the limbs of trees. This is to preserve them from the wolves, and to be used in time of need, when they are devoured, though rotten and full of maggots. The fish of the upper waters are said to be hardly edible, and, compared with those caught at the mouth of the Columbia, are totally different in flavour. The latter are the richest and most delicious fish I ever recollect to have tasted: if any thing, they were too fat to eat, and one can perceive a difference even in those taken at the Willamette Falls, which, however, are the best kind for salting. There are four different kinds of salmon, which frequent this river in different months: the latest appears in October, and is the only kind that frequents the Cowlitz river. The finest sort is a dark silvery fish, of large size, three or four feet long, and weighing forty or fifty pounds.

There is one point which seems to be still in doubt, namely, where the spawn of this fish is deposited. It is asserted, and generally believed, that none of the old fish ever return to the sea again. It has not been ascertained whether the young fry go to the ocean; and, if they do so, whether as spawn or young fish.

Mr. Drayton, during the time he remained at the falls, procured

[129]

a beautiful specimen of a small-sized sucker, which the Indians caught in their nets, and of which he made a drawing. The lamprey eels were also a source of curiosity: they seemed to increase in numbers, crawling up by suction an inch at a time. At these eels the boy who accompanied Mr. Drayton took pleasure in throwing stones, which excited the wrath of the Indians, as they said they should catch no more fish if he continued his sport. They have many superstitions connected with the salmon, and numerous practices growing out of these are religiously observed: thus, if any one dies in their lodges during the fishing season, they stop fishing for several days; if a horse crosses the ford, they are sure no more fish will be taken.

During the fishing season there are about seventy Indians, of both sexes, who tarry at the falls, although the actual residents are not, according to Mr. Waller, beyond fifteen. They dwell in lodges, which resemble those described heretofore, and are built of planks split from the pine trees. These are set up on end, forming one apartment, of from thirty to forty feet long, by about twenty wide. The roof has invariably a double pitch, and is made of cedar bark: the doorway is small, and either round or rounded at the top. I have mentioned that the outside is well stocked with fleas: it need scarcely be said what the condition of the inside is.

These Indians are to be seen lounging about or asleep in the daytime; but they generally pass their nights in gambling. Mr. Drayton, while at the falls, obtained a knowledge of some of their games. The women usually play during the day at a game resembling dice. The implements are made of the incisor teeth of the beaver, and four of these are used, which are engraved on two sides with different

figures, and the figures on two of the teeth are alike: these are taken in the hand and thrown on a mat, the players sitting on it, opposite to one another. They are of the shape represented in the cut. If all the blank sides come up, it counts nothing; if all the engraved or marked sides, it counts two; if two blanks and two differently marked sides, it counts nothing; but if two with like marks, it counts one. The game is generally twenty, which are marked with pieces of stick; the tens are noted with a smaller stick. This game is played for strings of dentalium [tooth-shells], called by them "ahikia;" each string is about two feet long, and will pass for considerable value, as the shells are difficult to procure: ten of them are said to be worth a beaver-skin.

The men and boys play a game with small bows and arrows: a wheel, about a foot in diameter, is wound round with grass, and is rolled over smooth ground; the players are divided into two parties: one rolls the wheel, while the other shoots the arrow at it. If he sticks his arrow into the wheel, he holds it on the ground edgewise towards the one who rolled it, who, if he shoots his arrow into it, wins his opponent's arrow; and this goes on by turns.

Another game is played by a party of men and boys, in the following manner: two poles are taken, six or eight feet long, and wound round with grass; these are set up about fifty feet apart. Each player has a spear, which he throws in his turn. Whichever side, after a number of throws, puts the greatest number of spears in their opponent's pole, wins the game. The usual bet among the men is a cotton shirt.

Mr. Drayton also paid a visit to the Indian village on the Klackamus river, which is about three miles from the falls, in company with Mr. Waller. The village is one and a half miles up the Klackamus, and its inhabitants number about forty-five individuals. Mr. Waller went there to preach, and about half the inhabitants of the village attended. The chief was the interpreter, and was thought to

[131]

have done his office in rather a waggish sort of manner. Preaching to the natives through an interpreter is at all times difficult, and especially so when the speaker has to do it in the Indian jargon of the country. This village has been disputed ground between Mr. Waller and Mr. Bachelét, the former claiming it as coming within his district. Not long before our visit, Mr. Bachelét had planted a staff and hoisted on it a flag bearing a cross. When this became known to Mr. Waller, he went to the place and pulled it down, and has driven Mr. Bachelét away. Such difficulties are very much to be deprecated, as they cannot but injure the general cause of Christianity in the eyes of the natives; and it is to be wished that they could be settled among the different sects without giving them such publicity; for the natives seldom fail to take advantage of these circumstances, and to draw conclusions unfavourable to both parties.

The men of the Klackamus village are rather taller and better-looking than the Clatsop or Chinook Indians: they belong to the Callapuya tribe. The women and children are most of them crippled and diseased. They have been quite a large tribe in former times, as is proved by the crowded state of their burying-ground, which covers quite a large space, and has a multitude of bones scattered around.

Their mode of burial is to dig a hole, in which the body is placed, with the clothes belonging to the individual: it is then covered up with earth, and a broad head-board is placed upright, of from two to six feet high, which is frequently painted or carved with grotesque figures: all the personal property of the deceased is placed upon this, consisting of wooden spoons, hats, tin kettles, beads, gun-barrels bent double, and tin pots. Although they are very superstitious about disturbing the articles belonging to the dead, yet all these have holes punched in them, to prevent their being of any use to others, or a temptation to their being taken off. It frequently hap-

[132]

pens that the head-boards will not hold all the articles, in which case sticks are used in addition. To rob their burying-grounds of bodies is attended with much danger, as they would not hesitate to kill any one who was discovered in the act of carrying off a skull or bones.

Of their medicine-men they have a great dread, and even of their bones after death. Thus, a medicine-man was buried near this burying-ground about a year before our visit to the country, whose body the wolves dug up: no one could be found to bury his bones again, and they were still to be seen bleaching on the surface of the ground.

It is no sinecure to be a medicine-man; and if they inspire dread in others, they are made to feel it themselves, being frequently obliged to pay the forfeit of their own lives, if they are not successful in curing their patients. The chief of the Klackamus tribe told Mr. Drayton that some of his men had gone to kill a medicine-man, in consequence of the death of his wife. These men afterwards returned with a horse and some smaller presents from the medicine-man, which he had paid to save his life.

This rule equally applies to the whites who prescribe for Indians, an instance of which occurred a short time before our arrival, when Mr. Black, a chief trader in one of the northern posts, was shot dead in his own room by an Indian to whose parent (a chief) he had been charitable enough to give some medicine. The chief died soon after taking it, and Mr. Black paid the forfeit of his kindness with his life. The deed was done in a remarkably bold and daring manner. The Indian went to the fort and desired to see Mr. Black, saying he was sick and cold. He was allowed to enter, and Mr. Black had a fire made for him, without any suspicion of his intentions. On his turning his back, however, towards the Indian, he was instantly shot, and fell dead on his face, when the man made his escape from the fort before any suspicions were excited of his being the murderer.

To Mr. Black the world is indebted for the greater part of the geographical knowledge which has been published of the country

[133]

west of the Rocky Mountains; and he not only devoted much of his time to this subject, but also to the making of many collections in the other departments of natural history, as well as in geology and mineralogy.

I remained at Vancouver till the morning of the 17th, and passed these few days with much pleasure in the company of the gentlemen of the fort, of whose attentions and great kindness I shall long entertain a grateful remembrance.

Mr. Waldron* now joined me from Astoria, without bringing any news of the Peacock or tender. I did not think it worth while to wait any longer their coming, when I had so much duty to perform elsewhere. After completing orders for Captain Hudson, I determined to return. Plumondon was sent to the Willamette Falls for Mr. Drayton, as I desired to have some consultation with him before my departure.

The day before I left the fort, Mr. Ogden informed me that he had made arrangements to take me as far as the Cowlitz Farm in his boat, on my way to Nisqually, and desired that I would allow Mr. Drayton to accompany him up the river as far as Wallawalla. To both of these arrangements I readily assented.

During my stay at Vancouver, I frequently saw Casenove, the chief of the Klackatack tribe. He lives in a lodge near the village of Vancouver, and has always been a warm friend to the whites. He was once lord of all this domain. His village was situated about six miles below Vancouver, on the north side of the river, and, within the last fifteen years, was quite populous: he then could muster four or five hundred warriors; but the ague and fever have, within a short space of time, swept off the whole tribe, and it is said that they all died within three weeks. He now stands alone, his land, tribe, and property all departed, and he left a dependant on the bounty of

*T. W. Waldron, of the crew of the *Porpoise,* who had been left at Astoria awaiting the overdue *Peacock.*

the Company. Casenove is about fifty years of age, and a noble and intelligent-looking Indian. At the fort he is always welcome, and is furnished with a plate at meal-times at the side-table. I could not but feel for the situation of one who, in the short space of a few years, has lost not only his property and importance, but his whole tribe and kindred, as I saw him quietly enter the apartment, wrapped in his blanket, and take his seat at the lonely board. He scarce seemed to attract the notice of any one, but ate his meal in silence, and retired. He has always been a great friend to the whites, and during the time of his prosperity was ever ready to search out and bring to punishment all those who committed depredations on strangers.

Casenove's tribe is not the only one that has suffered in this way; many others have been swept off entirely by this fatal disease, without leaving a single survivor to tell their melancholy tale.

The cause of this great mortality among the Indians has been attributed to the manner in which the disease has been treated, or rather to their superstitious practices. Their medicine-men and women are no better than jugglers, and use no medicine except some deleterious roots; while, from the character of these Indians, and their treatment of an unsuccessful practitioner, the whites decline administering any remedies, for fear of consequences like those to which I have alluded.

On the morning of the 17th, Vancouver was awake at an early hour, and preparations were actively making; a voyageur occasionally was to be seen, decked out in all his finery, feathers, and flowing ribands, tying on his ornamented leggins, sashes, and the usual worked tobacco-and-fire pouch. The latter is of the shape of a lady's reticule, and generally made of red or blue cloth, prettily worked with beads. In working them the wives of the officers of the Company exercise great taste, and it is deemed fully as essential a part of dress in a voyageur's wardrobe as in a lady's. The simple bag

[135]

does not, however, afford sufficient scope for ornament, and it has usually several long tails to it, which are worked with silk of gaudy colours.

The ladies of the country are dressed after our own bygone fashions, with the exception of leggins, made of red and blue cloth, richly ornamented. Their feet, which are small and pretty, are covered with worked moccasins. Many of them have a dignified look and carriage: their black eyes and hair, and brown ruddy complexion, combined with a pleasing expression, give them an air of independence and usefulness that one little expects to see. As wives, they are spoken of as most devoted, and many of them have performed deeds in the hour of danger and difficulty, worthy of being recorded. They understand the characters of Indians well.

About ten o'clock, we were all summoned to the great dining-hall by Dr. M'Laughlin, to take the parting cup customary in this country. When all were assembled, wine was poured out, and we drank to each other's welfare, prosperity, &c. This was truly a cup of good-fellowship and kind feeling. This hanging to old Scotch customs in the way it was done here is pleasant, and carries with it pleasing recollections, especially when there is that warmth of feeling with it, that there was on this occasion. After this was over, we formed quite a cavalcade to the river-side, which was now swollen to the top of its banks, and rushing by with irresistible force.

On reaching the river, we found one of Mr. Ogden's boats manned by fourteen voyageurs, all gaily dressed in their ribands and plumes; the former tied in large bunches of divers colours, with numerous ends floating in the breeze. The boat was somewhat of the model of our whale-boats, only much larger, and of the kind built expressly to accommodate the trade: they are provided yearly at Okonagan, and are constructed in a few days: they are clinker-built [with overlapping, or shiplap, boards], and all the timbers are flat. These boats are so light that they are easily carried across the

[136]

portages. They use the gum of the pine to cover them instead of pitch.

After having a hearty shake of the hand, Captain Varney, Mr. Ogden, and myself, embarked. The signal being given, we shoved off, and the voyageurs at once struck up one of their boat-songs. After paddling up the stream for some distance, we made a graceful sweep to reach the centre, and passed by the spectators with great animation. The boat and voyageurs seemed a fit object to grace the wide-flowing river. On we merrily went, while each voyageur in succession took up the song, and all joined in the chorus. In two hours and a half we reached the mouth of the Cowlitz, a distance of thirty-five miles.

In the Cowlitz we found a strong current to contend against, and by nightfall had only proceeded twelve miles further. As we encamped, the weather changed, and rain began to fall, which lasted till next morning.

I had much amusement in watching the voyageurs, who are as peculiar in their way as sailors. I was struck with their studious politeness and attention to each other, and their constant cheerfulness.

On the second day, our voyageurs had doffed their finery, and their hats were carefully covered with oiled skins. They thus appeared more prepared for hard work. The current became every mile more rapid, and the difficulty of surmounting it greater. The management of the boats in the rapids is dexterous and full of excitement, as well to the passengers as to the voyageurs themselves. The bowman is the most important man, giving all the directions, and is held responsible for the safety of the boat; and his keen eye and quick hand in the use of his paddle, delights and inspires a confidence in him in moments of danger that is given without stint. We did not make more than ten miles during the day, and were forced to encamp three miles below the farm.

On the 19th we reached our destination. On our approach, although there were no spectators, except a few Indians, to be expected, the voyageurs again mounted their finery, and gaily chaunted their boatsong.

Mr. Ogden had been one of the first who travelled over this part of country, and he informed me that he has seen the whole country inundated by the rise of the river. This, however, can but rarely occur, and could only be the result of a sudden melting of the snows when accompanied with violent rain-storms.

Plumondon had gone before, to request Mr. Forrest to send the wagon for our baggage; and we found it duly waiting at the landing.

In the afternoon, I made a visit, with Mr. Ogden, to the Catholic Mission, and several of the settlers' houses. That of Plumondon we found quite comfortable. The neighbourhood, though consisting of few families, appears very happy and united. They prefer the Cowlitz to the Willamette, although the land here is not so good as in the valley of the latter; but they say that many vegetables succeed here, that will not grow on the Willamette.

It was with much regret that I parted from Mr. Ogden and Captain Varney. We had enjoyed ourselves much, and I shall long remember their kindness and jovial company. The day they left us proved very rainy; it was impossible for any one to stir out, and the mud was ankle-deep. I felt disappointed at this, as I wished to make some observations, to test those I had already taken in passing before. Mr. Forrest was very attentive, and did all in his power to amuse me; but feeling disposed to sleep, I lay down, and after a short time awoke, with the feeling of having overslept myself. I jumped up to look at my pocket-chronometer, which, to be careful of, I had placed on the table. Lying near by it was a small silver watch, which I had not before observed, and my surprise was great to find that they both showed the same hour. I uttered my surprise aloud just as Mr. Forrest entered the room, and told me that he had

[138]

found my watch altogether wrong, (it showed Greenwich time,) and he had set it for me. I could not help making an exclamation of astonishment. We stood looking at each other, and he appeared fully as surprised as I was, when I told him that he had changed my Greenwich time for that of Cowlitz, and had interrupted my series of observations. He thought it passing strange that I should prefer Greenwich time to that of Cowlitz, and told me that he was sure his watch was right, for it kept time with the sun exactly! This incident, though sufficiently provoking at the time, afforded me much amusement after it was over, and was a lesson to me never to trust a chronometer to such an accident again.

It having partially cleared up the next morning, I set off accompanied by Plumondon, his wife and child, and another settler as my guide. We departed at eight o'clock, and being provided with good horses, made rapid progress. By the advice of Mr. Forrest, I endeavoured to take a canoe on the Chickeeles [Chehalis] sending the horses to meet us, without loads, over the mountain.

We rode up to the Indian lodges, near the Chickeeles river, in order to engage some of them to accompany us. I have before spoken of making a bargain with them, and of the time and patience necessary before any thing can be accomplished. I now saw that it was a hopeless task to attempt to overcome their perfect nonchalance. Time, haste, clothes, presents, are nothing to them; rum is the only thing that will move them at all times, and of this I had none, nor should I have made use of it if I had. When Plumondon had exhausted his words on them without effect, we rode off, succeeded in passing the mountain road quickly, and were well satisfied that we had thus shown our independence.

I have noticed the excessive love that the whole Indian population seem to have for rum: many of these poor creatures would labour for days, and submit to all sorts of fatigue, for the sake of a small quantity. No other inducement will move them in the salmon and

[139]

cammass seasons, for then they have nothing more to desire.

Towards night we encamped on a small prairie, where the grasses, flowers, and trees were in every variety of bloom.

The Indians on the Chickeeles river were engaged in the salmon-fishery. This is effected by staking the river across with poles, and constructing fikes or fish-holes, through which the fish are obliged to pass. Over these are erected triangles to support a staging, on which the Indians stand, with nets and spears, and take the fish as they attempt to pass through: the fish are then dried by smoking, and prepared for future use. The smoked fish are packed in baskets; but the supply is far short of their wants.

The next morning we set out early, and reached the opposite bank of Shute's river. On the following day before noon, I returned to Nisqually, fully as much enchanted with the beautiful park scenery as when I passed it before. To it was now added occasional peeps of Mount Rainier's high and snowy peak.

WALLAWALLA

ON MY RETURN to Nisqually, I found that news had been received from the various surveying and exploring parties, all of which it was reported were advancing rapidly in the execution of their duties. The preparations for the scientific operations, which had been left to the charge of Lieutenant Carr, were all completed, and the two log houses had been built, in which we now began to perform the pendulum experiments, and make astronomic observations. In these we were engaged until the 4th of July.

It was stated in the preceding chapter, that through Mr. Ogden's kindness, a passage was offered up the Columbia river as far as Wallawalla. It had been my original intention to despatch a party from the Peacock in this direction, to cross the Rocky Mountains to the head waters of Yellowstone river; and I had engaged a Mr. Rogers to accompany it. Orders for the purpose had been prepared, and left to be delivered to Captain Hudson [captain of the Peacock] when he should arrive.*

I now, however, began to apprehend that some serious accident had happened to that vessel, and I deemed it important to secure at all events, the examination of so interesting a part of this country, particularly when it could be performed under such favourable circumstances as those offered by Mr. Ogden. Mr. Drayton was therefore detached to make this jaunt, and to his industry and observation I am indebted for many of the facts about to be detailed. For others of them I have to acknowledge my obligation to the missionaries, and the officers of the Hudson Bay Company.

Previous to the departure of the brigade, Mr. Drayton had made

---

*Wilkes suffered much anxiety concerning the fate of the *Peacock* and at length became convinced that she had met with some sea disaster. His fears were confirmed, weeks later, on learning that the vessel had been sunk while attempting to enter the mouth of the Columbia on July 18. Her crew was saved.

many collections in natural history. After I left him, the weather continued very rainy for several days, and the Columbia in consequence began to rise again rapidly: the low prairies were overflowed, and the wheat in many places was injured. To show the porous nature of the soil, I will mention that the well at Vancouver rises and falls with the river, although it is a quarter of a mile from the bank. This is not the case in any other place in the territory where wells are sunk; but I have little doubt the same thing would occur on any of the low prairies of the Columbia, for the soil of all of them seems very similar. At Vancouver they use the river in preference to the well-water, though they do not consider the latter as unwholesome.

Mr. Drayton obtained in the mill-pond, specimens of a beautiful spotted trout, which is abundant there. They take the bait readily, and were caught with pieces of dried salmon: they feed upon insects, and small white moths are their favourite bait, at which they are seen to spring most greedily.

Until the 26th, repairs were making to the boats, and preparations were going on for embarking the goods. The shape of these boats has been before described: they have great strength and buoyancy, carry three tons weight, and have a crew of eight men, besides a padroon [steersman]: they are thirty feet long and five and a half feet beam, sharp at both ends, clinker-built, and have no knees. In building them, flat timbers of oak are bent to the requisite shape by steaming; they are bolted to a flat keel, at distances of a foot from each other: the planks are of cedar, and generally extend the whole length of the boat. The gunwale is of the same kind of wood, but the rowlocks are of birch. The peculiarity in the construction of these boats is that they are only riveted at each end with a strong rivet, and being well gummed, they have no occasion for nailing. They answer, and indeed are admirably adapted to, all the purposes for which they are intended; are so light as to be easily transported over the port-

[142]

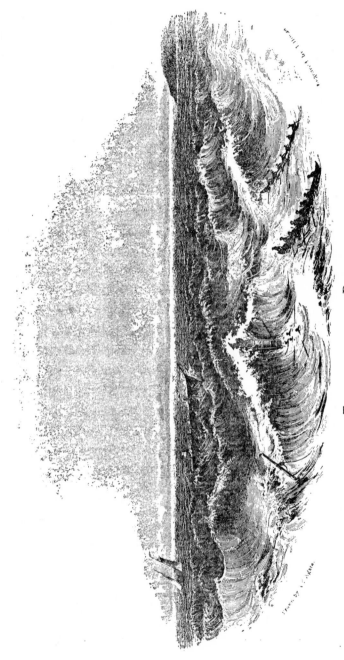

THE WRECK OF THE PEACOCK.

ages by their crews, and in case of accident are easily repaired.

The goods embarked for the supply of the northern posts are all done up carefully in bales of ninety pounds each, and consist of groceries, clothing, flour, powder, bullets, &c. It may readily be imagined that the different packages vary very materially in size, from a few inches square to two feet. This equal division of the weight is necessary, in consequence of the numerous portages they have to make, as well as convenient in forming packs for horses, which they take at Okonagan for a journey to Thompson river, which takes twenty days to accomplish.

Mr. Ogden is generally six months of every year travelling to and from his post on the south end of Stuart's Lake, called Fort St. James, in latitude 54° N. He leaves it early in the spring, and returns in the fall of each year. Before he departs, he fits out his summer trappers, and on his return those for the winter's campaign. He brings down with him the produce of a year's hunting. This post is the most profitable of all the sections west of the mountains. The average cost of a beaver-skin is about twenty-five cents, and when it reaches Vancouver it has enhanced in price to two dollars and fifty cents. The amount of furs brought down by Mr. Ogden yearly will net in London £50,000, a fact which will give some idea of the value of this trade.

In setting out on his journey, Mr. Ogden's practice, as well as that of all the Company's parties, is to go only a few miles the first day, in order that they may discover if any thing has been neglected, and be able to return for it. For this reason their first encampment was at the saw-mill. Their brigade consisted of nine boats, rowed by sixty voyageurs, eight of whom had their Indian wives with them. Besides these were Mr. and Mrs. M'Kinley, (Mr. Ogden's son-in-law,) who was to take charge of the Wallawalla Fort, and a Mr. Cameron, also of the Company, who was on his way to Mr. Black's station. The boats take each sixty packages, excepting the trader, which is Mr. Ogden's own boat, and carries only forty. The boatmen are Canadians, excepting about one-fourth, who are Iroquois Indians, all strong, active and hardy men. They are provided only with a square sail, as the wind blows generally either directly up or down the river.

On the 27th June, they were off at early dawn, took their breakfast at Prairie du Thé, and reached the Company's fishery, at the Cascades, at 6 P.M., where they encamped. This is the head of ship navigation, where the river takes a turn northward, and for upwards of two miles is comparatively narrow—four hundred and fifty yards wide. It falls in this distance about forty feet, and the whole body of water drives through this narrow channel with great impetuosity, forming high waves and fearful whirlpools, too dangerous to be encountered by any boat. When the river is low, these rapids are sometimes passed by skilful boatmen, but there have been many lives lost in the attempt.

The country bordering on the river is low until the Cascades are approached, with the exception of several high basaltic bluffs. Some of them are two hundred feet high, pointed like turreted castles.

An old Indian, called Slyboots, made his call upon Mr. Ogden for his annual present, consisting of some tobacco and a shirt. This present is made in consequence of his once having preserved Mr. Ogden's party from an attack, by giving information that it was to take place. By this timely notice Mr. Ogden was enabled to guard himself and party by taking refuge upon a small island just above the Cascades.

The Columbia, at this part, passes through the Cascade range of mountains between high and rocky banks. The geological character of this range is basaltic lava, basaltic conglomerate, and sandstone. Large quantities of petrified wood are to be found in the neighbourhood. Mr. Drayton obtained specimens of all of these.

The river, thus far, is navigated by seeking out the eddies. The

[145]

great difficulty is found in doubling the points which are at times impassable except by tracking [pulling with ropes] and poling. The oars are used after the French or Spanish fashion, adding the whole weight of the body to the strength of arm.

At the Cascades, during the fishing season, there are about three hundred Indians, only about one-tenth of whom are residents: they occupy three lodges; but there was formerly a large town here. Great quantities of fish are taken by them; and the manner of doing this resembles that at the Willamette Falls. They also construct canals, on a line parallel with the shore, with rocks and stones, for about fifty feet in length, through which the fish pass in order to avoid the strong current, and are here taken in great numbers.

There are two portages here, under the names of the new and the old. At the first, only half of the load is landed and the boats are tracked up for half a mile further, when the load is again shipped. The boats are then tracked to the old portage. A strong eddy occurs at this place, which runs in an opposite direction; and here it is necessary to land the whole of the cargo; after which the empty boats are again tracked three quarters of a mile beyond.

To a stranger unacquainted with the navigation of this river, the management of these boatmen becomes a source of wonder; for it is surprising how they can succeed in surmounting such rapids at all as the Cascades. Their mode of transporting the goods, and the facilities with which they do it, are equally novel. The load is secured on the back of a voyageur by a band which passes round the forehead and under and over the bale; he squats down, adjusts his load, and rises with ninety pounds on his back; another places ninety pounds more on the top, and off he trots, half bent, to the end of the portage. One of the gentlemen of the Company informed me that he had seen a voyageur carry six packages of ninety pounds each on his back (five hundred and forty pounds) ; but it was for a wager, and the distance was not more than one hundred yards. The voyageurs in

[146]

general have not the appearance of being very strong men. At these portages, the Indians assist for a small present of tobacco. The boats seldom escape injury in passing; and in consequence of that which they received on this occasion, the party was detained the rest of the day repairing damages.

On their starting next morning, they found that the boats leaked; and put on shore again to gum them. This operation, Mr. Drayton describes thus. On landing the goods, the boats are tracked up and turned bottom up, when they are suffered to dry; two flat-sided pieces of fire-wood, about two feet long, are then laid together, and put into the fire, until both are well lighted, and the wood burns readily at one end and in the space between; they then draw the lighted end slowly along the gummed seam, blowing at the same time between the sticks: this melts the gum, and a small spatula is used to smooth it off and render the seam quite tight. The common gum of the pine or hemlock is that used; and a supply is always carried with them.

A short distance above the Cascades they passed the locality of the sunken forest, which was at the time entirely submerged. Mr. Drayton, on his return, visited the place, and the water had fallen so much as to expose the stumps to view: they were of pine, and quite rotten, so much so that they broke when they were taken hold of. He is of opinion that the point on which the pine forest stands has been undermined by the great currents during the freshets; and that it has sunk bodily down until the trees were entirely submerged. The whole mass appears to be so matted together by the roots as to prevent their separation. Changes, by the same undermining process, were observed to be going on continually in other parts of the river.

On the 30th of June, they had a favourable wind, but it blew so hard that they were obliged to reef their sail, and afterwards found the waves and wind too heavy for them to run without great danger; they in consequence put on shore to wait until it abated. In these

[147]

forty miles of the river, it usually blows a gale from the westward in the summer season almost daily.

In the evening they reached within seven miles of the Dalles, and four below the mission. Here the roar of the water at the Dalles was heard distinctly.

The country had now assumed a different aspect; the trees began to decrease in number, and the land to look dry and burnt up. Before pitching their tents, the men were beating about the bushes to drive away the rattlesnakes, a number of which were killed and preserved as specimens.

In the morning they were again on their route, and reached Little river, from which the station of the Methodist Mission is three-fourths of a mile distant. Here they were met by Mr. Perkins, who was waiting for his letters and some packages of goods the brigade had brought. Mr. Drayton accompanied Mr. Perkins to the mission, while the brigade moved on towards the Dalles. Mr. Daniel Lee, the principal of the mission, was found near the house, reaping his wheat.

At this station there are three families, those of the Rev. Mr. Lee, Mr. Perkins, and a lay member, who is a farmer. Their reception of Mr. Drayton was exceedingly kind.

The mission consists of two log and board houses, hewn, sawed,

AN OREGON MISSION HOUSE.

and built by themselves, with a small barn, and several out-houses. The buildings are situated on high ground among scattered oaks, and immediately in the rear is an extensive wood of oaks and pines, with numerous sharp and jagged knolls and obelisk-looking pillars of conglomerate, interspersed among basaltic rocks: in front is an alluvial plain having a gradual descent towards the river, and extending to the right and left. This contains about two thousand acres of good land, well supplied with springs, with Little river, and other smaller streams passing through it. The soil is made up of decomposed conglomerate, and in places shows a deep black loam. Around this tract the land is high, devoid of moisture, and covered with basaltic rocks or sand.

They here raise wheat and potatoes by irrigation: the latter grow in great perfection, and wheat yields twenty to thirty bushels to the acre. They had just gathered a crop of two hundred bushels from land which they irrigate by means of several fine streams near their houses. They might raise much more if they were disposed. The summers here are much hotter than at Vancouver, and consequently drier; the spring rains cease here earlier, and the people harvest in June.

There are only a few Indians residing near the mission during the winter, and these are a very miserable set who live in holes in the ground, not unlike a clay oven, in order to keep warm. They are too lazy to cut wood for their fires. The number that visit the Dalles during the fishing season, is about fifteen hundred: these are from all the country round, and are generally the outlawed of the different villages. The missionaries complain much of the insolent behaviour and of the thieving habits, both of the visiters and those who reside permanently at the falls. They are, therefore, very desirous of having a few settlers near, that they may have some protection from this annoyance, as they are frequently under apprehension that their lives will be taken.

It is not to be expected that the missionaries could be able to make much progress with such a set, and they of course feel somewhat discouraged, though they have succeeded in obtaining a moral influence over a few.

The river between the Cascades and the Dalles, a distance of forty miles, has no rapids, and is navigable for vessels drawing twelve feet of water. It passes through high rocky banks of basalt.

The missionaries informed Mr. Drayton that the salmon-fishery at the Dalles lasts six months, and that sturgeon are taken during the greater part of the year.

The mission is three miles from the Dalles. On Mr. Drayton reaching the lower point of the portage, he found Mr. Ogden encamped, and a boat-load of packages spread out to dry. It appeared that one of the boats had bilged in passing up, and required repairs. The place was luckily fitted for these operations, as it had but one entrance to protect against about a thousand Indians, on the look-out for whatever they could pick up, and who required the whole force of the brigade to keep them in check.

The Dalles is appropriately called the Billingsgate [fish market] of Oregon. The diversity of dress among the men was greater even than in the crowds of natives as seen in the Polynesian islands; but they lack the decency and care of their persons which the islanders exhibit. The women also go nearly naked, for they wear little else than what may be termed a breech-cloth, of buckskin, which is black and filthy with dirt; and some have a part of a blanket. The children go entirely naked, the boys wearing nothing but a small string round the body. It is only necessary to say that some forty or fifty live in a temporary hut, twenty feet by twelve, constructed of poles, mats, and cedar bark, to give an idea of the degree of their civilization.

The men are engaged in fishing, and do nothing else. On the women falls all the work of skinning, cleaning, and drying the fish for their winter stores. As soon as the fish are caught, they are laid

[150]

FISHING HUTS AT THE DALLES.

for a few hours on the rocks in the hot sun, which permits the skins to be taken off with greater ease; the flesh is then stripped off the bones, mashed and pounded as fine as possible; it is then spread out on mats and placed upon frames to dry in the sun and wind, which effectually cures it; indeed, it is said that meat of any kind dried in this climate never becomes putrid. Three or four days are sufficient to dry a large matfull, four inches deep. The cured fish is then pounded into a long basket, which will contain about eighty pounds; put up in this way, if kept dry, it will keep for three years.

During the fishing season the Indians live entirely on the heads, hearts and offal of the salmon, which they string on sticks and roast over a small fire.

The fishing here is very much after the manner of that at Willamette Falls, except that there is no necessity for planks to stand on, as there are great conveniences at the Dalles for pursuing this fishery. They use the hooks and spears, attached to long poles: both the hook and the spear are made to unship readily, and are attached to the pole by a line four feet below its upper end. If the hook were made permanently fast to the end of the pole, it would be liable to break, and the large fish would be much more difficult to take. The Indians are seen standing along the walls of the canals in great numbers, fishing, and it is not uncommon for them to take twenty to

[151]

twenty-five salmon in an hour. When the river is at its greatest height, the water in the canals is about three feet below the top of the bank.

The Dalles is one of the most remarkable places upon the Columbia. The river is here compressed into a narrow channel, three hundred feet wide, and half a mile long; the walls are perpendicular, flat on the top, and composed of basalt; the river forms an elbow, being situated in an amphitheatre, extending several miles to the northwest, and closed in by a high basaltic wall. From appearances, one is led to conclude that in former times the river made a straight course over the whole; but, having the channel deeper, is now confined within the present limits. Mr. Drayton, on inquiry of an old Indian, through Mr. Ogden, learned that he believed that in the time of his forefathers they went up straight in their canoes. In order to illustrate this pass, Mr. Drayton made a careful diagram of it, which is represented in the wood-cut on the following page.

Besides the main channel, A, there are four or five other small canals, through which the water passes when the river is high: these are but a few feet across. The river falls about fifty feet in the distance of two miles, and the greatest rise between high and low water mark, is sixty-two feet. This great rise is caused by the accumulation of water in the river above, which is dammed by this narrow pass, and is constantly increasing, until it backs the waters and overflows many low grounds and islands above. The tremendous roar arising from the rushing of the river through this outlet, with the many whirlpools and eddies which it causes, may be more readily imagined than described.

The boat was repaired by the afternoon, and an express was despatched up the river to Wallawalla, in order to prepare the post for the reception of the brigade and inform the gentleman who had charge of it that he would be required to move to the north with the brigade. The officers of the Company have but little time allowed

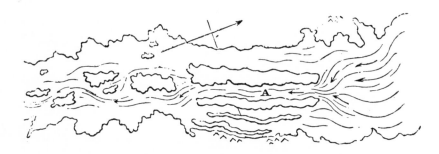

them to attend to their comforts: so completely are they under the control of accident, that they are liable to be called upon at any moment. Their rights, however, are looked to as much as possible, and the great principle adopted as the incentive to action is the advancement they may obtain by their own merit, through which alone they can get forward. In consequence of adhering to this principle, the Hudson Bay Company are always well served. The discipline that is preserved is the very best, and sits lightly upon all. Those who do not meet with advancement have some great fault in a trader's eyes. The enterprise and energy required to serve this Company well is of no ordinary kind, and few men exhibit more of both these qualities than those I met with in its employ.

On the morning of the 4th July, they began to pass the portage, which is a mile in length. It is very rugged, and the weather being exceedingly warm, many of the Indians were employed to transport articles on their horses, of which they have a large number. It required seventy men to transport the boats, which were carried over bottom upwards, the gunwale resting on the men's shoulders. By night all was safely transported, the boats newly gummed, and the encampment formed on a sandy beach. The sand, in consequence of the high wind, was blown about in great quantities, and every body and thing was literally covered with it.

From the high hills on the southern bank of the river there is an extensive view of the country to the south. The distant part of this prospect was made up of rolling, barren and arid hills. These hills, as well as the country nearer at hand, were covered with a natural hay or bunch-grass, which affords very nutritious food for cattle.

The missionaries have been stationed at the Dalles since 1838. The primary object of this mission is, in the first place, to give the Gospel to the Indians, and next to teach them such arts of civilization as shall enable them to improve their condition, and by degrees to become an enlightened community. There are many difficulties that the missionary has to contend with, in first coming among these people, none of which are greater than the want of knowledge of their true character. The missionaries, after a full opportunity of knowing these Indians, consider covetousness as their prevailing sin, which is exhibited in lying, dishonest traffic, gambling and horse-racing. Of the latter they are extremely fond, and are continually desirous of engaging in it. This sport frequently produces contentions which often end in bloodshed. Stealing prevails to an alarming extent: scarcely any thing that can be removed is safe. The missionaries have several times had their houses broken open, and their property more or less damaged. The stealing of horses in particular is very common, but after being broken down they are sometimes returned. There are but few chiefs to whom the appeal for redress can be made, and they can exercise but little control over such a lawless crew. Those who gather here are generally the very worst of the tribes around.

The number of Indians within the Dalles mission is reckoned at about two thousand; in but few of these, however, has any symptom of reform shown itself. They frequent the three great salmon-fisheries of the Columbia, the Dalles, Cascades, and Chutes, and a few were found at a salmon-fishery about twenty-five miles up the Chutes river.

The season for fishing salmon, which is the chief article of food in this country, lasts during five months, from May to September. The country also furnishes quantities of berries, nuts, roots, and game, consisting of bears, elk, and deer; but, owing to the improvidence of the native inhabitants, they are, notwithstanding this ample supply of articles of food, oftentimes on the verge of starvation.

After the fishing and trading season is over, they retire to their villages and pass the rest of the year in inactivity, consuming the food supplied by the labours of the preceding summer; and as the season for fishing comes round, they again resort to the fisheries. This is the ordinary course of life among these Indians, whose dissipation has been already spoken of and will claim more attention hereafter.

Here again some others demanded their annual token from the brigade for past services.

The country about the Dalles is broken, and the missionaries report that this is the case for some miles around. There are, however, also some plains and table-lands, which are considered as very valuable, being well watered with springs and small streams; excellent for grazing, and well supplied with timber—oak and pine. The soil varies in quality, and portions of it are very rich. Garden vegetables succeed, but require irrigation. Potatoes also must be watered, by which mode of culture they succeed well. Corn and peas can be raised in sufficient quantities. Wheat produces about twenty-five bushels to the acre: this is not, however, on the best land. They sow in October and March, and harvest begins towards the end of June.

The climate is considered healthy; the atmosphere is dry, and there are no dews. From May till November but little rain falls, but in winter they have much rain and snow. The cold is seldom great, although during the winter preceding our arrival the thermometer fell to -18° Fahrenheit. The greatest heat experienced in summer was 100° in the shade; but, even after the hottest days, the nights are cool and pleasant.

At daylight on the 3d July, the goods were all embarked. When they reached the Chutes, they again made a portage of their goods for a quarter of a mile, and in an hour and a half they were again on their way. During very high water, the fall, whence the place takes its name, is not visible, but when it is low there is a fall of ten feet perpendicular, that occupies nearly the whole breadth of the river. It is impossible to pass this fall at low water; but when the river is swollen, boats shoot it with ease and safety. The Columbia from the Chutes as far as John Day's river,* is filled with rocks which occasion dangerous rapids. The boats were in consequence tracked for the whole distance.

After passing the Dalles, an entirely new description of country is entered, for the line of woods extends no farther. The last tree stands on the south side of the river, and is named Ogden's Tree on our map: it is about six miles above the Dalles. The woods terminate at about the same distance from the coast in all parts of this region south of the parallel of 48° N.

The country between these places is decidedly volcanic, and the banks on either side of the river are rocky and high. In this part of the country it is very hot when there is no wind. Mr. Drayton had no thermometer, and therefore was unable to ascertain the exact degree of heat, but any metallic substance exposed to the sun for a short time could not be grasped in the hand without pain, and the men were almost exhausted with the heat.

There are a number of villages in this neighbourhood, and among them Wisham, mentioned in Irving's Astoria. This is situated on the left bank of the river, and its proper name is Niculuita; Wisham being the name of the old chief, long since dead. There are now in this village about forty good lodges built of split boards, with a roof of cedar bark, as before described. The Indians that live here seem

*Named for ex-Virginian John Day, a member of Wilson Price Hunt's overland party of 1810-12 for the founding of Astoria.

much superior to those of the other villages; they number four hundred regular inhabitants who live, like the rest, upon salmon; but they appeared to have more comforts about them than any we had yet seen.

At Niculuita Mr. Drayton obtained a drawing of a child's head that had just been released from its bandages, in order to secure its flattened head. Both the parents showed great delight at the success they had met with in effecting this distortion. The wood-cuts give a correct idea of the child's appearance.

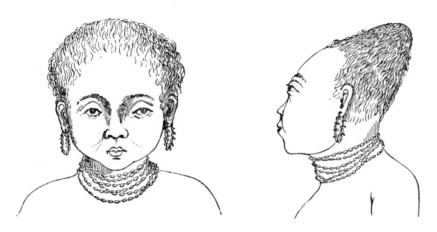

There were from fifty to one hundred Indians constantly following the brigade, and aiding the men. The price for half an hour's service was generally two leaves of tobacco, which was sought after with great eagerness. These Indians paint their faces with red and yellow clay. Their women seemed to be of more consequence than is usual among savages, and some of them even took command over the men.

At John Day's river great quantities of salmon are taken, and there are, in consequence, many temporary lodges here. Notwithstanding this is a rocky region, there are vast quantities of fine sand deposited every where, which is brought down the river. On this the encamp-ments are necessarily made; and the sand is exceedingly dry and hot, which renders the camping disagreeable. There are few places more uncomfortable; for a basaltic wall rises nine hundred or a thousand feet within two hundred yards of the camp, which reflects the sun's rays down upon the beach of white sand, rendering the atmosphere almost insupportable. To give some idea of the heat, Mr. Drayton found it uncomfortably hot to sit down upon the rocks an hour after the sun had set.

One of their amusements at the time of encamping was a rattle-snake hunt, in which several large ones were killed.

The brigade, as usual, set out early, and with the sun there arose a fine breeze, which carried them briskly onwards. About eight miles above their encampment they came to the Hieroglyphic Rocks. These are about twenty feet high, and on them are supposed to be recorded the deeds of some former tribe. They passed so quickly that Mr. Drayton could make only two hasty sketches of them; and it is to be regretted that they were not sufficiently perfect to allow of their being given in this place.

After passing John Day's river the country becomes much lower and more arid, and the current comparatively less. The weather was exceedingly hot, and the drifting sands were in greater quantities than before, so much so that whole islands were passed entirely composed of the sand. They now arrived at the long reach, just below Grand Island; the country becoming sandy and so flat as to give a view of the Grand Rapid Hills. It has the appearance of having been, at no very remote period, the bed of an extensive lake. Here the voyageurs began to be relieved from their toil at the pole, which they exchanged for the tow-line and oar, and the Indians departed the moment their services were no longer wanted. The distance made this day was fifty-seven miles, for which they were indebted to the breeze. The day before, they made only sixteen miles.

While passing close along the banks they met with numerous pin-

[158]

tailed grouse, so tame as to allow the boats to approach within a few feet of them before they would fly.

At their encampment Mr. Drayton found a large burying-place, from which he was desirous of getting a skull; but to the surprise of the party, several Indians made their appearance and prevented it. The corpses were placed above ground, in their clothing, and then sewed up in a skin or blanket; and the personal property of each deceased individual was placed near the body: over all were laid a few boards, of native construction, placed as a kind of shed to protect them from the weather.

All along this river from the Dalles up, there is not a piece of wood growing, and except occasionally a drift log, there is nothing larger than a splinter to be found. All the wood used for cooking is bought from the Indians, who will follow the brigade for many miles with a long pole or piece of a log, which they sell for a small piece of tobacco. The Indians also brought for sale several hares, which were large and of extremely fine flavour.

The country continues to be, as far as can be seen on every side, a barren and sterile waste, covered with a white sand mixed with rounded and washed pebbles. All that it produces is a little grass, some wood, and a species of small Cactus, filled with long white spines so hard and sharp that if trodden upon they will penetrate the leather of a boot.

On the 6th of July the brigade reached the foot of the Grand Rapids, up which the boats were tracked. They afterwards passed along the foot of Grand Rapid Hills, which are composed of basalt, old lava, and scoriae. These hills are steep on the river side, and are fast crumbling away and falling into the stream.

Eighteen miles below Wallawalla they passed the Windmill Rock, about which are a number of curious basaltic peaks. On approaching Wallawalla the scenery becomes grand: the country is broken into volcanic peaks, forming many fantastic shapes resembling

[159]

figures and colossal heads: many of them are seen either insulated or in groups; some of them are known under the name of the Nine-pins. Through this pass of volcanic rocks the wind rushes with great violence in summer, to supply the rarefied portion above. The current had increased very considerably: it often became necessary for the voyageurs to take a pipe, or in other words, a rest. When the brigade was in sight from the fort the Company's flag was hoisted. Before arriving there, and within a mile and a half of it, the country becomes again flat, and rises very little above the river when the water is high. The ground is composed of pebbles and drifting sand for several miles to the east and to the north, with little or no soil, and nothing grows on it but a few spears of bunch-grass and wormwood.

The brigade reached the fort at sunset, when they were received by Mr. M'Lean, who was in temporary charge of the post: and who reported himself ready to proceed with his Indian wife and children with Mr. Ogden; and Mr. M'Kinley took charge of Fort Wallawalla.

Fort Wallawalla is about two hundred feet square and is built of pickets, with a gallery or staging [platform] on the inside, whence the pickets may be looked over. It has two bastions, one on the south-west and the other on the northeast. On the inside are several buildings constructed of logs and mud; one of these is the Indian store: the whole is covered with sand and dust, which is blown about in

FORT WALLAWALLA.

[160]

vast quantities. The climate is hot; and every thing about the fort seemed so dry that it appeared as if a single spark would ignite the whole and reduce it to ashes.

The party under Lieutenant Johnson had passed by about a week previously, on their return to Nisqually.

At all the principal stopping-places, one or two old Indians would present themselves to Mr. Ogden to demand their annual present for services rendered him and the Company.

Many years back, Mr. Ogden, while on his route, was attacked at the place where the fort stands, by the Wallawalla tribe, and was obliged to take refuge on the island near the fort where he made a stand and completely routed the Indians. This occurrence took place twenty-three years before and was the cause of this post being occupied; since which time, no attack has been made.

This will give some idea of the dangers the officers and men of the Hudson Bay Company have to encounter; and although it is now safe on the Columbia river, yet there are many parts where they are still subject to these attacks: the voyageurs have a lot of toil and deprivation, yet few men are to be found so cheerful.

Mr. Ogden informed me that the most experienced voyageur is taken as a pilot for the brigade, and he is the bowman of the leading boat; which is looked upon as a station of great trust and honour. Each boat has also its bowman, who is considered the first officer and responsible man; the safety of the boat, in descending rapids particularly, depends upon him and the padroon, who steers the boat. They both use long and large blade-paddles; and it is surprising how much power the two can exert over the direction of the boat. These men, from long training, become very expert and acquire a coolness and disregard of danger that claim admiration and astonishes those who are unused to such scenes.

To all appearance, there is seldom to be found a more laborious set of men; nor one so willing, particularly when their remuneration

[161]

of no more than seventeen pounds sterling a year, and the fare they receive, are considered. The latter would be considered with us incapable of supporting any human being. It consists of coarse unbolted bread, dried salmon, fat (tallow), and dried peas. I am satisfied that no American would submit to such food: the Canadian and Iroquois Indians use it without murmuring, except to strangers, to whom they complain much of their scanty pay and food. The discipline is strict, and of an arbitrary kind; yet they do not find fault with it. Very few of those who embark or join this Company's service ever leave the part of the country they have been employed in; for after the expiration of the first five years, they usually enlist for three more. This service of eight years in a life of so much adventure and hazard, attaches them to it, and they generally continue until they become old men; when, being married, and having families by Indian women, they retire under the auspices of the Company to some small farm, either on the Red or Columbia rivers. There is no allowance stipulated for their wives or children; but one is usually made if they have been useful. If a man dies leaving a family, although the Company is not under any obligation to provide for them, they are generally taken care of. The officers of the Company are particularly strict in preventing its servants from deserting their wives; and none can abandon them without much secrecy and cunning. In cases of this sort, the individual is arrested and kept under restraint until he binds himself with security not to desert his family [again]. The chief officers of the Company hold the power of magistrates over their own people; and are bound to send fugitives or criminals back to Canada for trial, where the courts take cognizance of the offences. This perhaps is as salutary and effectual a preventive against crime as could be found, even if the courts were at hand; for whether innocent or guilty, the individual must suffer great loss by being dragged from the little property he possesses. The community of old voyageurs settled in Oregon are

[162]

thus constrained to keep a strict watch upon their behaviour; and, although perhaps against their inclinations, are obliged to conform to the wishes of those whose employ they have left.

The brigade, after remaining at Wallawalla till the 8th, took their departure. In taking leave of Mr. Ogden, I must express the great indebtedness I am under for his attentions and kindness to Mr. Drayton, as well as for the facility he offered him for obtaining information during their progress up the Columbia. I am also under obligations to him for much interesting information respecting this country, which he gave without hesitation or reserve. He was anxious that Mr. Drayton should accompany him to Okonagan; but as this route had just been traversed by another party, it would have been a waste of the short time he had to spend about Wallawalla. Mr. Ogden is a general favourite; and there is so much hilarity and such a fund of amusement about him, that one is extremely fortunate to fall into his company.

After the departure of the brigade Mr. Drayton set out to visit Dr. [Marcus] Whitman [at Waiilaptu], in company with Mr. M'Lean, who was to proceed to Okonagan with horses, to join Mr. Ogden. They rode about twenty miles before dark, and passed over some of the pastures of the horses belonging to the Company. An alluvial bank, one hundred feet in height, was pointed out, over which the wolves had driven part of a band of the horses of the Company by surrounding them just before dark. This took place some months before, and the horses were killed and eaten by these voracious animals. The wolves are very numerous in this country and exceedingly troublesome.

The country passed over on the banks of the Wallawalla, and within half a mile of it, was green and fertile. This will also apply to the banks of the small tributaries falling into the Wallawalla. To the north and south are extensive prairies covered with the natural hay of the country, on which the cattle feed; here these grasses spring up in the early spring rains, grow luxuriantly and are afterwards converted into hay by the great heat of the month of July. Thus dried, they retain all their juices. Of this hay the cattle are exceedingly fond, and prefer it even to the young grass of the meadows bordering the stream.

The party reached the mission about dark and were welcomed by Dr. Whitman and Mr. and Mrs. [William H.] Gray, of the American Board of Missions. This station was established in 1837, with three others, and is known by the name of Waiilaptu. The second station, called Lapwai (clear water), is at the mouth of the Kooskooskee, under the Rev. Mr. [Henry] Spalding. The third was about sixty miles up that river, and was called Kamia, where the Rev. Mr. [Asa] Smith was stationed for two years; finding, however, that he had no Indians to teach, or within reach of his station, he abandoned it. The fourth, called Chimikaine, is near the river Spokane, under the direction of Messrs. [Cushing] Eels and [Elkanah] Walker, sixty miles south of Colville.

At Waiilaptu there are two houses, each of one story, built of adobes, with mud roofs, to insure a cooler habitation in summer. There are also a small saw-mill and some grist-mills at this place, moved by water. All the premises look very comfortable. They have a fine kitchen-garden, in which grow all the vegetables raised in the United States, and several kinds of fine melons. The wheat, some of which stood seven feet high, was in full head and nearly ripe; Indian corn was in tassel, and some of it measured nine feet in height. They will reap this year about three hundred bushels of wheat, with a quantity of corn and potatoes. The soil, in the vicinity of the small streams, is a rich black loam and very deep. The land fit for cultivation along these streams does not, however, amount to more than ten thousand acres. This quantity is susceptible of irrigation and in consequence can be made to yield most luxuriant crops. In many parts of it a natural irrigation seems to take place

[164]

owing to the numerous bends of the small streams, which almost convert portions of the land into islands. These streams take their rise in the Blue Mountains about forty miles east of Wallawalla, and are never known to fail. The climate is very dry, as it seldom rains for seven or eight months in the year. During the greater part of this time the country forty miles north and south of this strip has an arid appearance. There are large herds of horses owned by the Indians that find excellent pasturage in the natural hay on its surface.

There is a vast quantity and profusion of edible berries on the banks of the streams above spoken of, consisting of the service-berry, two kinds of currants, whortleberry and wild gooseberries: these the Indians gather in large quantities for their winter supplies.

At the time of Mr. Drayton's visit there were at the mission only fourteen Indians, including men, women and children. Those who usually reside here had gone to the Grande Ronde to trade, a distance of twenty-five miles.

The Grande Ronde is a plain or mountain prairie surrounded by high basaltic walls. This is called by the Indians, "Karpkarp," which is translated into Balm of Gilead. Its direction from Wallawalla is east-southeast, and the road to the United States passes through it. It is fifteen miles long by twelve wide; and is the place where the Cayuse, Nez Percé and Wallawalla Indians meet to trade with the Snakes or Shoshones, for roots, skin lodges, elk and buffalo meat, in exchange for salmon and horses.

Mr. Drayton met with an old Indian at Waiilaptu who was pointed out as the man who took the first flag that was ever seen in the country to the Grande Ronde, as the emblem of peace. Lewis and Clarke, when in this country, presented an American flag to the Cayuse tribe, calling it a flag of peace; this tribe, in alliance with the Wallawallas, had up to that time been always at war with the Shoshones or Snakes. After it became known among the Snakes that such a flag existed, a party of Cayuse and Wallawallas took the flag and planted it at the Grande Ronde, the old man above spoken of being the bearer. The result has been that these two tribes have ever since been at peace with the Snakes, and all three have met annually in this place to trade. Dr. Whitman confirmed the old man's statement from other evidence he had received. The Grande Ronde is likewise resorted to for the large quantities of cammass-root that grow there, which constitutes, as I have before remarked, a favourite food with all the Indians.

These missionaries live quite comfortably, and seem contented; they are, however, not free from apprehension of Indian depredations. Dr. Whitman, being an unusually large and athletic man, is held in much respect by the Indians, and they have made use of his services as a physician, which does not seem to carry with it so much danger here as among the tribes in the lower country or farther north.

These missionaries have quite a number of cattle and horses, which require little or no attention, there being an abundance of hay and grass. The price of a good horse is twenty dollars.

This district is capable of supporting a vast number of cattle. One Cayuse chief has more than a thousand horses on these feeding grounds.

The winters are of about three months' duration and snow lasts only a short time; the grass indeed grows all winter. A better idea of the climate here may be formed from the fact, that Mr. M'Kinley, of the Hudson Bay Company, who passed from the Snake country across the Blue Mountains in January, 1841, found the snow on the mountains five and six feet deep, and the weather very cold; but when he descended to these plains the next day, the weather was warm and pleasant, the grass green, and many flowers in bloom.

On the Wallawalla river, trees are again met with: they consist of the poplar, willow, birch and alder. The poplar grows to the height of one hundred feet and has a diameter near the base of two and a half feet.

[166]

As respects the success of the missionary labours, it is very small here. The Indians are disposed to wander, and seldom continue more than three or four months in the same place. After they return from the Grande Ronde, which is in July, they remain for three or four months, and then move off to the north and east to hunt buffalo. After their return from the buffalo-hunt, they are again stationary for a short time.

Dr. Whitman has one hundred and twenty-four on his rolls, male and female, that receive instruction in the course of the year. He preaches to them on the Sabbath, when the Indians are on the Walla-walla river.

The school consists of about twenty-five scholars daily, and there appears some little disposition to improve in these Indians. The great aim of the missionaries is to teach them that they may obtain a sufficient quantity of food by cultivating the ground. Many families of Indians now have patches of wheat, corn and potatoes, growing well, and a number of these are to be seen near the Mission farm.

The Indians have learned the necessity of irrigating their crops, by finding that Dr. Whitman's succeeded better than their own. They therefore desired to take some of the water from his trenches instead of making new ones of their own, which he very naturally refused. They then dug trenches for themselves, and stopped up the Doctor's. This had well-nigh produced much difficulty; but finally they were made to understand that there was enough water for both, and they now use it with as much success as the missionaries.

There is much small game in this part of the country, which is easily obtained with a gun or by snares. The most numerous are the grouse, curlew, and two species of hare.

In company with Mr. Gray, Mr. Drayton visited the Blue Mountains. Before reaching the foot of the mountains they passed through large bands of horses belonging to the Cayuse Indians; the soil became better, being of a red colour, and formed of decomposed scoria. Much scoria is here seen in every direction and the grass in such places, from receiving more moisture, is more luxuriant. Mr. Drayton ascended up as far as the snow-line but had not the means of ascertaining his altitude; it was, however, from my observations, about five thousand six hundred feet. They here found the forest of pines, and the temperature was quite low. From this point the Wallawalla, with its numerous branches, could be seen threading its way through the plains beneath to unite itself with the Columbia river, yet more distant.

They returned the next day to Fort Wallawalla.

There seems to be a peculiarity about the climate at Wallawalla, not readily to be accounted for. It has been stated above that little winter weather is experienced there, and that this mildness is owing to the hot winds of the south, which sweep along from the extensive sandy deserts existing in Upper California. This wind, or simoon, during the summer, is held in great dread in this part of the country, for it is of a burning character that is quite overpowering. It generally comes from the southwest. In consequence of this feature of the climate there is very little vegetation near the fort, not only on account of the heat and dryness, but owing to the vast clouds of drifting sand, which are frequently so great as to darken the sky. In summer it blows here constantly, and at night the wind generally amounts to a gale. Mr. Drayton represents his situation in the northeast bastion of the fort as quite uncomfortable, from the fear of its being blown down.

The Indian mode of taking salmon was witnessed at this place. It consists in the erection of a fish-weir of basket-work, supported by poles. This is placed across the stream, in the form of an acute angle. This barrier dams the water sufficiently to create a little fall. The salmon swim up the river at night, and when they reach the barrier, they jump over the low side, which is down stream, but are unable to leap the higher one. A little before daylight the Indians spread their nets, carefully avoiding to disturb the fish about the weir, and take all those that have been ensnared. These usually amount to about twenty-five.

Small parties of the Cayuse, Wallawallas and Nez Percés were now returning from the Grande Ronde. They occupied about thirty lodges made of poles, mats, and skins bought from the Shoshones.

During the week, the Columbia had fallen ten feet. It is here one thousand yards wide, and the altitude of Fort Wallawalla above the sea is twelve hundred and eighty-six feet.

The proximity of these Indians afforded Mr. Drayton an opportunity of observing them, and having an Indian boy with him, who understood both their language and English, he had no difficulty in communicating with them.

The chief of the Wallawallas, who is called Puipui-Marmax (Yellow-Bird) and the Nez Percé chief Touwatui, (or Young Chief,) seemed intelligent and friendly, but the white residents consider them as great rogues. They were going to the Shaste country* to trade for blankets, powder and ball, together with trinkets and beads, in exchange for their horses and beaver-skins.

The Company, and the settlers of the Willamette, refuse to trade either powder or ball in this country, and it is but a short time since the Indians have been able to obtain any. The reason assigned by the Company and residents for this restriction is that the natives become quarrelsome and turbulent when they are provided with fire-arms. On these trips they are accompanied by about thirty warriors, well armed.

The men are usually clothed in blanket coats; but, notwithstanding this slight approximation to civilized habits, they have the air of the Indian, strongly marked, about them.

The number of Indians now collected was two hundred. The

---

*The Shaste (Shasta) country was comprised of southern Oregon including part of the Rogue River valley, and a portion of northern California. The district was not under close control of the Hudson's Bay Company.

women were employed in drying salmon and the cammass-root. Some of them are employed in cooking while others are engaged in dressing skins.

MALE COSTUME.

The mode of removing the hair from the skins is with a round and broad chisel, fixed on a handle, like an adze: the skin, while yet green, is laid on a log or board and the hair chopped off. The smoking process differs from that already described at the Cowlitz. A large hole is dug in the ground in which a fire is made; the skin is sewed on the inside of a bag, which is suspended immediately over the fire, so that little of the smoke can escape, and the process goes on rapidly. This process is necessary, otherwise it would, on becoming wet, and drying afterwards, be hard and stiff.

There were many children among these people. The young Indian women as well as the wives of the Company's servants who have married half-breeds, invariably use a long board as a cradle, on

[170]

which the child is strapped, and then hung up on a branch, or to the saddle. When travelling, a hoop, bent over the head of the child, protects it from injury. The women are usually dressed in skins very much ornamented with beads.

FEMALE COSTUME.

Mr. Drayton, during his stay, was attracted one day by the sound of beating sticks and a kind of unearthly singing, issuing from one of the lodges. On going to the lodge he found a boy about eighteen years of age lying on his back, very ill, and in the last stage of disease. Over him stood a medicine-woman, an old haggard-looking squaw, under great excitement, singing as follows:

hi tu e oo ha ha hi tu e oo ha ha ha ha ha ha—ha ha ha ha.

To which shout a dozen men and boys were beating time on the sticks, and singing a kind of bass or tenor accompaniment. The

[171]

words made use of by the old squaw varied, and were any that would suit the case. She bent over the sick boy and was constantly in motion, making all kinds of grimaces. She would bare his chest, and pretend by her actions to be scooping out his disease; then she would fall on her knees and again strive to draw out the bad spirit with both hands, blowing into them and, as it were, tossing the spirit into the air.

The evening of the same day, Mr. Drayton paid another visit to the same lodge, when he found the medicine-squaw much exhausted. She was blowing with her mouth on his neck downwards, making a quick sputtering noise, thus—

hi   tu   e   ah   tut - t - t - t - tut, tut - t - t - t - tut.

While she was uttering this, a man was holding her up by a rope tied round her waist, while she, bending over the body, began to suck his neck and chest in different parts, in order more effectually to extract the bad spirit. She would every now and then seem to obtain some of the disease, and then faint away. On the next morning she was still found sucking the boy's chest, and would frequently spit into her hand a mouthful of saliva and blood, which she had extracted from her own gums, and spread it with her finger over the palm of her hand, taking great care that all should see it. She would then pronounce the boy better, with apparent satisfaction. So powerful was the influence operated on the boy, that he indeed seemed better, and made endeavours to speak. The last time Mr. Drayton visited the doctress, her patient was found sitting up. She exhibited a stone, about the size of a goose's egg, saying she had taken the disease of the boy out of him as large as it, and that he would now get well. The parents were greatly delighted to hear that their son would recover. The reward she was to receive was a large basket of

[172]

AN INDIAN LODGE IN WALLAWALLA COUNTRY.

dried salmon, weighing eighty pounds, a blanket, and some other presents.

One singular custom prevailing here is, that all the convalescent sick are directed to sing for several hours during the day.

It would be a profitable occupation to be a medicine-man or woman, were it not for the forfeiture in case of want of success; but this applies only where the patient is a person of distinction.

It is seldom that medicine-squaws are met with, as they are by no means numerous.

It was observed that many of the females were living under a little hut at some distance from the lodges; and it was ascertained that women during the menstrual period are not allowed to remain in the lodges, and are obliged to stay in huts at a distance, managing the best way they can during its continuance. This custom also prevailed very strictly after childbirth, and in that case continues for forty days. This latter custom, however, is not so rigidly adhered to by this tribe, at present, as it used to be; but among the northern tribes it is very strictly observed.

By the 20th, Mr. Drayton had finished his drawing and sketching,

[173]

and obtained the necessary data for the map of the river and the country surrounding this post, to which it was one of the most central, and a commanding one for the protection of the country; and as I deemed that accurate information respecting it would be desirable, I had directed his attention particularly to this business. The manner in which this task was executed was very satisfactory, and merits my warmest acknowledgments.

In company with Mr. M'Kinley, Mr. Drayton rode to the great forks of the Columbia. On reaching that place, they made their way up the south branch, which is a large stream, and navigable for canoes a short distance above the mouth of the Kooskooskee river.

A remarkable phenomenon occurs on the junction of the waters of the Columbia and Snake rivers: the Columbia from the north brings a cold current, while the Snake from the south is warm. This difference is perceived even at Wallawalla; for the water passing along the east shore near the fort is too warm to drink, and when they desire to have cool water for drinking it is brought from the middle of the river by a canoe.

On the day that Mr. Drayton was to leave Wallawalla, four men, who had accompanied Mr. Ogden's brigade as far as Okonagan, returned to Wallawalla on their way back to Vancouver. They brought no letters from Mr. Ogden.

Mr. M'Kinley furnished Mr. Drayton with horses, and Indian guides to return with the horses from the Dalles, and the party was increased by the four voyageurs to the number of eight. By the kindness of Mr. M'Kinley, and by the direction of Mr. Ogden, Mr. Drayton found himself fitted with good horses and every convenience requisite for the journey, besides a quantity of provisions. The first night they encamped near the Windmill Rock, having travelled a distance of thirteen miles.

The voyageurs, however, were found destitute of almost every thing, and spoke of their having been furnished with only a little

[174]

tobacco, to carry them from Okonagan to Vancouver. Knowing Mr. Ogden's character as I do, I cannot believe that such was the fact. There were some, however, found by Mr. Drayton destitute of every thing, and he provided these with supper from his own stores, after which they lay down on the ground to sleep without any shelter whatever. The general impression is, that these men are badly found and cared for.

They chose the left or south bank of the Columbia for their descent. Although the road on the north is the shortest, that on the south is better. In passing along, trails are seen, many sometimes joining together; which mark the routes of the Indians in their journeys across the country.

The next night they encamped within fifteen miles of John Day's river. Near their encampment there were several lodges containing about forty Indians. At sunset, at the lodge of the old chief, a little bell was rung, when they all repaired thither and joined in devotions, the leader praying very loud. On the prayer being finished, they commenced gambling, and kept it up all night; but when the sun rose they again resorted to the lodge of the chief for prayer as before. During the whole night they made a most tremendous noise, singing and beating with sticks on splintered rails, which is the only substitute they have for a musical instrument.

The country had been easily travelled over until John Day's river was approached, when the route became extremely rough and rocky. On the banks of that river is a large village of about sixty Indians, and they were ferried across the stream for a pound of tobacco, while the horses swam over.

These Indians were as great extortioners as the others and demanded tobacco, powder, and ball. The latter articles they are most desirous of obtaining, as the possession of them enables them to visit their hunting-grounds at the foot of Mount Hood.

The musquitoes were again found here in numbers; but the upper country seems to be entirely free from that annoyance.

The country from this ferry to the Chutes river is a flat prairie, half a mile wide, high enough not to be overflowed and tolerably well watered, overgrown with small grass. The party passed the Chutes river before sunset, and encamped on its western bank.

On the morning of the 24th, they reached the Dalles. Mr. Drayton found this place entirely altered in its appearance, so much so that he could hardly realize that it was the same. The water had fallen during the twenty days of his absence, about thirty feet, and was still subsiding. The Columbia was now confined within high perpendicular rocks; the beach, where he had before stood, and been able to touch the water with his hand as it passed through the confined banks, was now far above it, and the river, instead of rushing through its many canals, was now confined to a single one. It still, however, rushed along with all the fury and violence of a mighty torrent, and had yet as much as twenty-seven feet to fall to low water. In this state of the river the Company's boats frequently shoot or descend it, but this is at all times an exploit of great danger. Many fearful accidents have taken place with the most experienced boatmen, who with all their skill could not preserve themselves from being carried into the vortices, drawn under, and destroyed.

Such is the peculiar nature of the rush of waters through the Dalles, that for some minutes the whole will appear quite smooth, gliding onwards as though there were no treachery within its flow, when suddenly the waters will begin to move in extended and slow whirls, gradually increasing in velocity until it narrows itself into almost a funnel shape, when, having drawn towards it all within its reach, it suddenly engulfs the whole, and again resumes its tranquil state.

An awful accident was related to me by Mr. Ogden, of which he was an eye-witness, which will more clearly illustrate the nature of the place.

[176]

Mr. Ogden was descending the river in one of the Company's boats with ten Canadian voyageurs, all well experienced in their duties. On arriving at the Dalles, they deemed it practicable to run them, in order to save the portage. Mr. Ogden determined, however, that he would pass the portage on foot, believing, however, the river was in such a state that it was quite safe for the boat to pass down. He was accordingly landed, and ascended the rocks, from which he had a full view of the water beneath, and of the boat in its passage. At first she seemed to skim over the waters like the flight of a bird; but he soon perceived her stop, and the struggle of the oarsmen, together with the anxious shout of the bowman, soon told him that they had encountered the whirl. Strongly they plied their oars, and deep anxiety if not fear was expressed in their movements. They began to move, not forwards, but onwards with the whirl: round they swept with increasing velocity, still struggling to avoid the now evident fate that awaited them: a few more turns, each more rapid than the last, until they reached the centre, when, in an instant, the boat with all her crew disappeared. So short had been the struggle, that it was with difficulty Mr. Ogden could realize that all had perished. Only one body out of the ten was afterwards found at the bottom of the Dalles, torn and mangled by the strife it had gone through.

Mr. Drayton found that as many as half of the Indians had left their fishing. He noticed here, in attempting to make a bargain for canoes to take him as far as the Cascades, the same habit of extortion that was before evinced. In all cases, it seems to be a part of the Indian character to take advantage of distresses and wants. He was finally obliged to give four times as much as it ought to have cost to execute the work; and after the bargain was made, they informed him they must be paid before they launched the canoe; and when that was done, a fathom of tobacco must be given to each of them for launching her. This demand was not complied with, and the goods that had been paid were now seized and taken away again. Mr. Drayton then

[177]

proceeded to the mission, where Mr. Lee kindly offered his canoe. This was accordingly put on an ox-cart,—for it is necessary to keep it near his house to prevent its being stolen,—and carried to the water. When they reached the river, the two canoes above spoken of were seen near the landing-place, and the owners offered them for a much less price, and without any "potlatch." Their offer was then accepted, when he embarked, and proceeded down the river about twelve miles, where they encamped.

At daylight the next morning there was not an Indian to be found, and two of the best paddles were gone, as well as the men's salmon. On a search being made, the fish were found hidden in the bushes. After leaving the shore, they were called to by the Indian, and on returning to him, the only excuse he offered was, that he had been asleep, and had but just awoke: he, however, ran off into the bush again. After they joined the other canoe, the old Indian in it said that the one who had run away had endeavoured to persuade him to steal Mr. Drayton's things; and when they landed at night the plan was to take the canoe and all off, when he was on shore: this was prevented by their carefully putting all the things into the tent.

When they reached the Cascades, an examination was made of the pine stumps before spoken of.

The same evening a boat reached the salmon-fishery, by which Mr. Drayton returned to Vancouver, where he met with the same kind reception and welcome he had before received.

From this trip, Mr. Drayton brought with him the materials for the construction of a map of the river, above the Cascades as far as Wallawalla, which has been incorporated in our chart of Oregon. I take this occasion to say that I have embraced within this the whole of the territory of Oregon between the parallels of 42° and 54° N. The southern pass of the Rocky Mountains is also included, which was taken from the surveys of Lieutenant Frémont, of the United States Engineer Corps, and which I have designated as Frémont's Pass. This officer is now engaged in an exploration of the country about the Youta Lake and the middle section of the territory, in a line on the east of the Cascade Range, from John Day's river to the south,—a portion of the country it was my intention to have traversed, if the Peacock had reached the Columbia river at the appointed time.

OF THE ILLUSTRATIONS

THE Oregon Book Society is indebted to Dr. Stephen Dow
Beckham of McMinnville, Oregon, for permission to repro-
duce the illustrations in this book. Found in Volume IV of
the Wilkes *Narrative*, all of these drawings appear to have been
executed by Mr. J. Drayton, except *The Wreck of the Peacock*
which is credited to Mr. Agate. Both artists were among the
corps of "learned gentlemen" who accompanied the Wilkes
Expedition.

COLOPHON

THE TEXT of this book was set in Linotype Bodoni Book type at the Inland Press at Ashland, Oregon. Types for display matter were composed in Caslon faces, and the printing of the pages was performed at The Private Press of Lewis Osborne at Laurel Hill, Ashland. The paper is Curtis Rag. The binding, in Columbia Mills' Bolton buckram, was done at The Filmer Brothers Press at San Francisco.